A Prisoner of Stalin

A Prisoner of Stalin

The Chilling Story of a Luftwaffe
Pilot Shot Down and Captured on the
Eastern Front

Christian Huber

FRONTLINE
BOOKS

An imprint of
Pen & Sword Books Ltd
Yorkshire – Philadelphia

FRONTLINE
BOOKS

Originally published in Germany, as *Vom Himmel in die Hölle*, 2015 by Rosenheimer Verlagshaus
First published in Great Britain in 2022 by
FRONTLINE BOOKS
an imprint of Pen & Sword Books Ltd,
47 Church Street, Barnsley, S. Yorkshire, S70 2AS

ISBN: 978-1-52673-321-4

CIP data records for this title are available from the British Library

For more information on our books, please visit
www.frontline-books.com, email info@frontline-books.com
or write to us at the above address.

Printed and bound by CPI Group (UK) Ltd, Croydon, CR0 4YY
Typeset by Concept, Huddersfield, West Yorkshire

Pen & Sword Books Ltd incorporates the imprints of Pen & Sword
Archaeology, Atlas, Aviation, Battleground, Discovery,
Family History, History, Maritime, Military, Naval, Politics,
Social History, Transport, True Crime, Claymore Press,
Frontline Books, Praetorian Press,
Seaforth Publishing and White Owl

For a complete list of Pen and Sword titles please contact
PEN & SWORD LTD
47 Church Street, Barnsley, South Yorkshire, S70 2AS, England
E-mail: enquiries@pen-and-sword.co.uk

Or

PEN AND SWORD BOOKS
1950 Lawrence Rd, Havertown, PA 19083, USA
E-mail: Uspen-and-sword@casematepublishers.com

To my wife Angela

Disclaimer

The course of military events corresponds to historical truth. The names of the persons mentioned are to the largest extent authentic.

Gerhard Ehlert belongs to the few survivors of an elite Luftwaffe unit that undertook night-time reconnaissance sorties over the Russian regions during the Second World War. Although he came from a parental home that was against the Nazi regime, he volunteered. Ehlert completed twenty-two operational sorties, often landing his aircraft blindly in fog. However, in June 1944 he was shot down and taken prisoner by the Russians. His time in the camps changed his life forever.

This eyewitness description is based on the recollections of a surviving German Luftwaffe officer.

Contents

HISTORICAL NOTE

At 17.00 hours on 14 June 1944, Leutnant Gerhard Ehlert and his crew from 2. Nachtaufklärungsstaffel were assigned to take photos of the railway and roads around Sarny following an attack the previous night. They took off from Baranowitschi in a Do 217M-1 coded K7+FK, apparently the personal aircraft of their Staffelkapitän Hauptmann Paul Palmer, at around 21.30 hours and headed east. Approaching the target, they climbed to an altitude of 1,500m and prepared to take photographs by using flash bombs, but the bomb doors did not open, so they went down to 200m for visual reconnaissance and reported via radio.

However, on their return flight the Beobachter, Oberfeldwebel Hanns Schlotter, became unsure of their location. The aircraft then flew into the range of a Soviet flak battery which opened fire and quickly damaged the rudder. The last message that Luftflotte 2 heard from Ehlert and his crew was at 01.15 hours.

The right engine had been hit first and burst into flame. The Dornier slowed down and gradually lost altitude. Ehlert was sitting in the front on the left, behind him the Bordmechaniker, about 50cm higher than the Beobachter. This meant that their feet were not injured when they hit the ground, but the Beobachter, who sat lower in the cockpit, had his legs torn off in the crash-landing and he died almost immediately. Shrapnel had also hit the cockpit and mortally wounded the Bordfunker, Unteroffizier Karl-Heinz Williges, but Ehlert had managed to land in the Pripet Marshes. He was able to climb out and Feldwebel Wilhelm Burr, the Bordmechaniker, also got out of the burning wreckage but with severe burns to hands and face.

Both survivors wanted to get to the German lines, some 60 km to the west. Resting by day and walking at night they struggled on. On the second day they attempted to get some food in a small village, but villagers informed Soviet soldiers and they were soon captured.

Gerhard Ehlert did not return home until December 1949.

Chris Goss

1

Flight Without Return

Calmly the young pilot pulls the joystick towards himself. The heavy aircraft dips its nose slightly and the two Daimler-Benz engines show their mettle. The warm summer air flows beneath the wings of the twin-engine aircraft and lifts it gently. Gravity presses the men into their seats, and they feel entirely safe when they hear the retracting undercarriage click into place. They now feel the vibrations caused by the propellers in their lightweight suits, which are made of a light-coloured summer fabric that they learn to love during these hot days in the Pripet swamps. Due to these they sweat much less than their comrades in the thick grey uniforms. The humming of the engines radiates through to their skin and they feel it all over their bodies. And thus they head out into the dusk to the accompaniment of loud roaring. The last rays of the Russian sun trail behind them and die down, before they and their pterosaur are cloaked completely by the night. Their black bird, which can hardly be detected from the ground at night, has enough fuel for six hours. Three hours out, three hours back.

'Turn right. Straight. Up there in front, slight turn left. Straight!' the observer murmurs at second intervals into his throat microphone. He is crouching inside the huge glass cockpit below the pilot and has the best view down. 'This is like being in a Mercedes Silver Arrow driving at 300 kilometres an hour on the motorway; just with a black blindfold', smirks the aerial gunner, who is sitting at the very back of the narrow aircraft and as usual has nothing to do. At night the Russian fighters do not take off from their airfields; unlike the Tommies, they still do not have radar in summer 1944.

'It's almost a little lonely up here. Music wouldn't be bad now', crackles throatily in the headphones of the four men in their humming long-range reconnaissance plane. Then the gunner looks at his wristwatch: 'Oh professor, what about that radio message? Those at home need to know that we're still alive.'

The professor's name is actually Unteroffizier Karl-Heinz Williges. He is the baby of the crew and is on his first real combat flight sortie. The men call him the professor because he wears glasses and appears hugely intelligent because of them. He is having difficulty fighting off tiredness and his thoughts of home, of his mother. He has slept badly again during the day because his memories of the last training sortie near the front are still haunting him.

'Man, don't have a kip here. Anyone who can't handle this should let it be', the pilot scolds him, and Williges knows that he will not be permitted many mistakes otherwise he will be out. 'Out' means out of the cockpit and off to join the trench warriors. Trench warriors are what the 'gentlemen of the Luftwaffe' call infantry soldiers, whose demise is near during these days – at least here at the Pripet river south-east of Minsk – where three years earlier Hitler and the generals under his spell had gained one victory after another. The great cauldron battles near Kiev, in which the Red Army had lost hundreds of thousands of soldiers to death or captivity, the conquest of the route Minsk–Smolensk–Moscow, the rapid advance in the south toward the Crimea close to the Caucasian oilfields; all this had led to hubris on the German side. It was a hubris that one year and two winters later ended at the ice-cold Volga in the disaster of Stalingrad, where the German 6th Army was resoundingly defeated by the Red Army. It was the turning point of the war in the East, no, of the entire war of destruction into which Hitler's Germany had dragged Europe and half the globe.

On the Eastern Front during these summer days of 1944 a storm is brewing. Now a seamless front of the German Wehrmacht only exists on paper. The once so victorious Army Group Centre has bled out on the way from Moscow to Minsk. The Red Army is gathering for the crucial offensive and now with a wholly new, threatening undertone. For the first time since the invasion of the Wehrmacht into Soviet Russia a nerve-wracking humming from the air is added to the wearing artillery preparation of the Russians: 1,000 Soviet bombers target the remains of the German front line for days. Luftflotte 6 can provide just forty operational fighters to Army Group Centre at this time. Forty aircraft against 1,000. Straight into the preparations of the Red Army flies this single German plane on the evening of 13 June at around 9.30pm. It is one of the last night-time reconnaissance planes in the Luftwaffe. The mission reads: reconnaissance of the railway and roads in the area of the 2nd Army.

What the crew see during this night on their sortie no longer surprises them and yet still chills their blood. These are the omens of doom. Train after train rolls toward the West, pulled by heavy, steaming locomotives, loaded with tanks and ordnance. In the Russian staging areas are so many of the dreaded T-34 tanks, assault guns and Katyushas that it looks as if the fields consist of pure steel. Fields of iron, meadows of lead. On the roads at night they see truck convoy after truck convoy. They are driving with headlights blazing, such is their faith in their safety. The men in the reconnaissance plane know that once at the front the transporters will spit out Red Army soldiers, thousands, a million and more. And they know that their comrades on the ground will not be able to stem this flood. Not for a single day. For the Russians, there are now only 300km left until East Prussia.

Leutnant Gerhard Ehlert, the pilot of aircraft 'K7+FK', has a bad feeling. Although he is concentrating on following the instructions of his observer, he still has time to reflect now and again. And reflection is what he needs the least. It renders him distracted. He worries about Riele, his girl at home, and recalls her features from his memory again and again. It makes him smile. He thinks of her brown hair, smelling it in his thoughts, and cannot explain to himself why he has not heard anything from her for two weeks. It is most likely the fault of the goddam field postal service. He calms himself and is jolted out of his thoughts.

'Sharp left turn, Leutnant Sir, steeper. Straight. Up there in front, right turn. Attention. Now. Straight!' the observer yells again and again. They are flying according to the map. That means the observer – Oberfeldwebel Hanns Schlotter from Frankfurt am Main – correlates what he recognises with his naked eye on the ground to his map in front of him. Second by second. And that in the middle of the night. He has no time for thoughts during the flight, otherwise they will lose their way and possibly end up in an area with strong air defences. That is the last thing they need. And just as the tall, wiry observer zones out for two seconds, the cold and vibrating voice of his pilot reaches his ears. 'Schlotter. You all right? I hear too little. Man, use your eyes, otherwise we will lose our way here', Ehlert yells harshly.

Schlotter is immediately wide awake again. 'Yes Sir, Leutnant Sir. Along the river, straight, right turn. Straight. Up there in front, another sharp right turn. Attention: now! Straight!' Schlotter at once functions like a machine again, just like their twin-engine Dornier Do 217.

The young Leutnant at the joystick senses, however, that a peculiar tension has fallen over the entire crew today. Perhaps it is quite good in this case to steady the situation a little, he thinks to himself. 'Williges! Do you actually know where the word *verfranzen* [to lose one's way] derives from? It's aviator slang from the World War.' He does not give a number to the world war, the first, for Ehlert does not know that the one they are currently fighting will receive the number two.

'In the aircraft of the World War one man was seated at the front and one in the back. The names given to those two aviators were Emil and Franz. Emil piloted, Franz navigated, just like Schlotter right now, only slightly slower. If they lost their way, Franz had made a mistake and they were *verfranzt*. But this won't happen to us, right, Schlotter?'

'Yessir, Leutnant Sir. Right turn. Straight. Ahead a slight left turn. Straight!' Schlotter replies.

What a clever clogs is our coachman today, thinks Willi Burr, the bored gunner at the tail of the machine. The latter is now being pulled slightly upwards by Ehlert, because Schlotter warned him of a range of hills. 'The planes then were more like swings. They plunged down in droves. We won't lose the sky, right, Burr? No machine is as airworthy as ours if we fly it right.'

'Yessir, Leutnant Sir, none!', the gunner answers reconciled.

Altitude 200m. Below the four men in the Do 217, shadows pass by in a mad rush and paint bizarre shapes on roads, meadows and fields. Sometimes the moon casts the shadow of Gerhard Ehlert's reconnaissance plane onto a woodland clearing and they pass by their own shadow. Again and again they see the lights of trucks. An ocean of lights merging into one bright glow. The Russians have long since gained absolute air superiority and no longer need to worry their heads about German fighters. Barely any more at least. Therefore they no longer need blackouts. 'This is like Christmas,' Burr bellows, and at the same time Williges sends his half-hourly radio message to their airfield.

During these days the German army command could already see the writing on the wall and what the Red Army was planning: a large-scale attack towards East Prussia scheduled to commence on 22 June 1944. In order to disrupt the preparations, for weeks the last aircraft of the Luftwaffe have been mainly attacking train stations, either in small groups or on desperate solo missions. One of them is Sarny Station, which on 13 June was bombarded by the few remaining aircraft of Luftflotte 6. Sarny is situated on the Kiev–Warsaw line about 300km west of Kiev and equidistant from Minsk.

During the mission briefing at 5pm Ehlert and his crew are assigned to photograph the track system the night after the bombardment. The squadron commander uses a long, thin wooden stick to point at a map on the wall in front of them. He draws the flight route along rivers, railway tracks and roads. How easy it looks on this map and with a wooden stick, Ehlert thinks, and looks at the shadow cast by the stick. It points across Warsaw to Germany. Not a good omen! Aviators are superstitious. Nobody likes to board a plane with the designation thirteen. Some squadrons repaint them before the first mission as twelve and a half.

For their mission tonight Ehlert's men are assigned the squadron commander's plane, which is equipped with a special ISCO camera. With it they can take pictures of wide areas from a great height.

Two hours later the young lieutenant is having dinner with his fellow officer Kurt Schuffert in front of a tent at the front-line Baranovichi airstrip. The two talk casually about the fact that no machine has been lost for quite some time. Ehlert does not know yet that it will be his crew who will not return this night. We have not been not in the game long enough, we won't buy it yet, thinks Ehlert, who believes in the law of probability. And he knows that, apart from the youngster Williges, his crew has already had a lot of experience, especially Schlotter, the old warhorse. The latter is already in his thirties. Ehlert is not surprised that during war men who are by rights still young are considered old. Schlotter, Burr and I are the best prescription for a long life, he smiles to himself full of confidence. That is like a law to him. Yet war does not abide by laws – apart from those of death.

At 9pm their plane, a Dornier Do 217 M with twin engines that produce 3,000 hp, is fuelled. Then they take off toward Sarny. The approach goes smoothly at first. They glide low over the battlefield, which seems to be especially calm today. Only now and again do they see the illumination of muzzle flashes. Then it becomes quiet, and the radio decreases in volume. They are above enemy territory, penetrating almost 100m deeper every second. If they continue like this, they will reach Sarny in half an hour. Before that, however, they decide to have a little fun, just like it has been their habit during the past few days.

In a prominent forest clearing along the Kovel–Sarny train line, four Russian anti-aircraft guns are mounted in a square. What makes them special is the fact that they are operated by women. Three times already Ehlert and his men have seen the white of the eyes of the female crew, because every time they have descended very low shortly before reaching the emplacement. The lower they fly, the shorter the time they spend directly above the position. The low-level flyover of the German aircraft means that the Russian anti-aircraft crew gets into a right flap every time. The women run to and fro like startled chickens and do not manage to fire a single shot in time. And Ehlert's men are shouting, because they are having a blast watching the women in their earth brown uniforms dash about below. Even the usually cool pilot lets himself get carried away and wiggles the wings briefly before departing from the anti-aircraft emplacement. This gesture is the ultimate, bloodless penalty for the female trench warriors in the clearing below. For the wing wiggling means nothing but 'Sod you!' The women will think of a way of exacting revenge. This very night.

The mood quickly drops again inside Ehlert's aircraft. They cannot carry out their first objective. Shortly before Sarny Station they climb to 1,500m in order to take pictures under flashlights. Yet the bomb door, out of which the flashlight bombs are supposed to be dropped, cannot be opened. Burr leaves his gun in the tail of the plane and climbs down.

'I'll take a look at what's going on, Leutnant Sir!' the sergeant croaks into his microphone. All his wrenching, kicking and shoving does no good, though. The bloody door simply refuses to budge. Upside down, the aerial gunner drops a pencil from his breast pocket. The impact of the small pencil on the lower part of the plane's glass cockpit cannot be heard. It dances on top of the glass and will continue to do so for another half hour.

'Bomb door cannot be opened manually, either. Cannot be fixed by means on board, Leutnant Sir', Burr communicates to his pilot. Thus there will not be any photos from high altitude. This will not be the last mishap to befall aircraft K7+FK.

Ehlert slowly steers his bird in a wide, curving descent. They go down to 200m, their typical reconnaissance altitude. Now they have to count cars, trains and tanks. Oberfeldwebel Schlotter announces the direction and counts, Unteroffizier Williges radios to the airfield every half an hour and also counts. Feldwebel Burr covers their backs with his MG 131 as always, and Ehlert – the cabby as they call him – flies his bird stolidly and by the book. Now the four of them are a machine within a machine, a clockwork mechanism inside which every cog is capable and has to rely on the other. A band of brothers in arms. And although the fidgety professor, the gangly Oberfeldwebel with the keen eyes and crooked nose, the nonchalant sergeant with his machine gun and the cool, almost always slightly too formal pilot could not be more different from each other as personalities, they are wedded by one thought – that of home.

In Frankfurt am Main, Hanni Schlotter resides with her two sons. Fritz is three years old, Max only just a year old. The boys' father is at the front. No, even worse, behind enemy lines. Inside a flying coffin. In Mergelstetten, near Heidenheim, Linda is sitting on the bank of the little romantic River Brenz. She is wearing a white, sleeveless summer dress and is very tanned. She is twenty years old and has her whole life still in front of her. Her long blonde hair is tucked behind her ears, just a single lock falls into her eyes. With her radiant smile revealing a row of gleaming white teeth, she casts a spell on all those around her. With her high cheek bones, her chiselled features and her feminine figure she could have any man here in Mergelstetten. Yet she only wants one; Burr, the crazy Luftwaffe sergeant who flies around at night and who covers his comrades' backs inside the Do 217 with his cannon, as he calls his machine gun. And then there is Riele, who is everything to Gerhard Ehlert, the stern pilot with his crisp uniform.

Just in the minute in which the men inside the reconnaissance plane turn around above Sarny, Riele is holding Gerhard's picture in her hands. The visor cap makes him seem taller than he is, she thinks. He is tall and slim, and his uniform is without frills. Gerhard has no taste for especially debonair accessories like the kerchiefs or buckles that are commonly worn by pilots. This does not fit with the rule book, so he leaves them off.

And then there is the mother. Williges' mother. She has already lost her husband during the French campaign. He was one of the first casualties, has given his life 'for the Leader, the people and the fatherland'. She cannot get these words from the death notice out of her head any more, and they burn into her mind like the clear, individual notes of a fugue. A death fugue! When she thinks of her youngest son, Karl-Heinz, who flies with the Luftwaffe across Russia by night, she hears the fugue clearly. It is well that she does not know how her husband actually died, there at the Marne. It was a piece of shrapnel. When the medical orderly found him, he initially thought that the French had been shooting tomatoes. Everywhere was red with little yellow dots. The shrapnel had torn the skull into shreds. After this loss, Williges' mother would not be able to bear the death of one of her three sons. Most of all, not that of her youngest, who has always been so attached to his mother – more than to his father.

The crew's altitude is 200m. All instruments are working. The pencil is dancing inside the dome. The engines are humming evenly and quietly. 'Straight, right turn. Straight. Up there another right turn. Attention, straight!' Schlotter is reading the map, announcing the direction, Ehlert is flying and thinks of Riele.

'Are we carrying out our little joke again, Lieutenant Sir?' asks Burr over the radio. 'The Russian ladies run around so charmingly.'

Ehlert, however, no longer has the taste for fun. He wants to be home. 'Chauffeuring' for more than five hours in the air is draining his strength. As pilot he has the most taxing task of all four: to listen to the navigator, to concentrate, to keep the instruments in view, to fly the bird, to give orders to the crew. And he has the overall responsibility, which prohibits him undertaking something just for fun during this bloody war. He rarely breaks this rule. Tonight he has already let himself be carried away to do so and was immediately cross with himself. This will not happen a second time during this flight, he has sworn to himself immediately after his wave with the wings above the women's anti-aircraft emplacement. Ehlert wants to fly home, just home. Home to the dusty airfield near Baranovichi, drop off the film at the evaluation office, doss down and simply sleep until tomorrow, until the day after tomorrow, for a thousand days.

'We will be flying the shortest route. Twice green when we pass the main line of battle. Understood, Burr?'

'Yes Sir twice a green flare', the gunner replies. He operates the built-in flare gun under the fuselage of the aircraft. He is supposed to fire two green flares above the front line when entering their own airspace. This is the signal for the infantry below that it is one of their own planes soaring above them.

Another ten minutes, Burr is thinking to himself, then we are through with these bollocks again. Nearly there. And all is quiet. Too quiet. Burr hears the voice of Schlotter, who is still spouting directional information in a steady flow. Something seems to bother Schlotter, though. He sometimes hesitates for the fraction of a second, clears his throat. Falls silent for a couple of seconds. This is highly unusual for him.

'Schlotter', Ehlert shouts, 'I need directions, damn it! Pull yourself together, man!'

All three of them now realise that there is something wrong with the Oberfeldwebel. Small droplets of cold sweat dance across Williges' forehead to the same rhythm as the pencil below in the glass cockpit.

'360 degrees, Leutnant Sir', Schlotter gasps. 'Sod it, I've lost my orientation, Lieutenant Sir.' Three hundred and sixty degrees means that the pilot is supposed to circle until the observer regains orientation. Circling bodes ill. A plane is at the lowest risk of being spotted and brought down if it covers distance rapidly and keeps moving. Circling means a standstill. Below, the lights of the columns of trucks rush past. It will not be long until the hum of the German plane will be heard. And pulling up to a higher altitude is of no use, either. Then Schlotter will lose his orientation completely.

It takes a minute or two, an eternity, during which Schlotter is desperately looking back and forth between his map and the ground below, becoming more and more frantic. Damn, he thinks. His eyes hurt. The constant back and forth between the light below and the darkness above strains the pupils too much. Damn, the lake ought to be here. Nothing, and again nothing. Forest, no lake.

'I'll make another turn. Just a little one', Ehlert announces in a calm voice. It would do no good if he started to get nervous now, too. 'Perhaps we will spot something familiar.'

And indeed, there it is! There is the train line leading back to Baranovichi. Is it really the one? Yes, they divine the forest clearing and the low chain of hills. There must be the women's anti-aircraft emplacement close by, too. Ehlert actually wanted to avoid their guns. Oh well, he thinks, we'd better stick with it before Schlotter loses his orientation again. Those down there will be sleeping again anyway.

Yet this time the pilot is wrong with his assumption. The Russian battery commander has long since received the message from her infantry that a big black German bird is circling close to her position. This must be the German who made fun of them a few hours before. Now *we* will have fun with him, the Red Army soldiers below are thinking. They cling to their guns ready to fire and wait for their orders. And Ehlert does not know another important thing, something fatal. In a few seconds the scales will fall from his eyes. Too late he will register that they will not fly over the anti-aircraft emplacement in a direct pass from east to west, but transversely across the entire belt of Russian anti-aircraft emplacements. When they recognise the first white clouds of explosions in the night sky around them and their aircraft is seized by a heavy shockwave for the first time, they are still some kilometres away from the women's anti-aircraft position. Ehlert senses that all hell will break loose soon. He thinks of Riele and of home. The pencil inside the glass dome makes wild leaps.

2

Ashes

Ehlert's plane will soon erupt into flames and burn to ashes. Strangely enough, he is thinking about ashes – the ashes on which his home village Meiersberg was founded, after glass works had been burning wood for centuries. He would like to be back there right now. Four years – that is how long his last visit dates back. He thinks of his brother, his playmate of his earliest years, of his strict but amiable father who was a military musician, and of his mother who had warned him and everyone who would listen to her about the Nazis, and who for that reason was shunned in her village. Ehlert thinks of the time of his last summer holiday in Meiersberg before his entry into the Wehrmacht.

Back then he travelled to Ferdinandshof, the nearest large town to Meiersberg, in order to research his genealogy. To delve into one's own ancestry was very much the fashion in the dark empire of Heinrich Himmler. The Reich Leader SS had even launched a special office in which high-ranking officers and their assistants whiled away the time with racial science and genealogy for ideological purposes. So it was not surprising that throughout the entire Nazi empire people began to take an interest in their family history. For that reason, young Gerhard delved into the church records of Ferdinandshof, for which he had previously obtained official permission from the parish. As some of his ancestors had belonged to the founding families of Meiersberg in 1749, among the farmers on his father's side and among the glass makers on his mother's side, Gerhard found pages upon pages about his ancestors. For days he trawled through the books and turned pale from staying indoors so much despite the splendid late autumn in the Uckermark. Yet afterwards he knew where he came from, and that gave him a feeling of security.

In Meiersberg wide roads lead through the little village; roads that are too wide, the lanes separated by an even wider strip of greenery interspersed with tall trees – a kind of central promenade, as is usually found along the boulevards of big cities. Due to the wide and empty roads the houses opposite each other are wide apart. There is enough building ground here, and there is no need to skimp. Meiersberg is situated in Western Pomerania at the southern edge of the forest region of the Ueckermünde Heath. After the glaciers of the last ice age had retreated 10,000 years ago, they left behind a landscape with plenty of space: lakes, boulders, and most of all large areas of sand, not everywhere, but predominantly. Before humans settled there, the region consisted only of primordial forest interspersed with bogs, swamps and many little streams.

The village itself was only founded in 1749. Originally it consisted of two separate settlements but in spring that year a glass works started operations, and in the following summer farmers arrived, who set up their farmsteads immediately west of the glass works settlement. Before the founding of Meiersberg there was already a dairy in the vicinity with the peculiar name of Better Off. The two houses belonging to the dairy stood where the log canal flows into the River Zarow. Members of a family called Gundelach led the setting up of the glass works in Ferdinandshof and Meiersberg, and they were ancestors of Albert Ehlert and his two sons, Konrad and Gerhard.

One evening, the war, which had begun the previous year with the invasion of Poland, made a stop in Meiersberg – more by chance than through ill intention. Gerhard had been able to borrow some books for his research, because the sexton of the Ferdinandshof parish trusted him by now, after Gerhard and he had had the odd chat. The former was the first to hear the war arriving and grumpily glanced up from his church records. A low hum approached from the east and became increasingly louder.

By that time Gerhard had already decided to join the Luftwaffe, a decision not forced upon him by anyone, but which was fed mainly by the literature that the young man devoured greedily. He read books like *A Fight for Rome* (a historical novel by Felix Dahn published in 1876 and very popular as young adult fiction for several generations), not the adventure page-turners by Karl May (a best-selling author of the late nineteenth/early twentieth century mostly known for his fictional travel books set in the Wild West and the Middle East) like his friends. He was most impressed by books on the First World War, and also books by aviators. Yet at that time this was nothing but youthful enthusiasm. His real passion for aviation and for the life of a soldier was only awakened in him by the euphoric Wehrmacht reports of the first months of war. The Polish army had been 'squashed' by German dive bomber wings, and the Battle of Britain was in full swing and 'practically impossible to lose'. Germany would 'coventrate' English cities one by one, the Minister for Propaganda Josef Goebbels promised, after the Luftwaffe had carpet-bombed the English city of Coventry and virtually 'erased' it. Victory after victory, gained by aviators!

Gerhard wanted to become a pilot, a fighter pilot, even though he had never even flown in a glider like many of his later comrades. Only then could one have assumed that his passion for flying was a logical step. For Gerhard it was the language, the words in the books, which brought him to flying. He told his parents of his intention to join the Luftwaffe during one Sunday morning breakfast in spring 1940. Father and mother had no objections. The topic was dealt with in just one minute, the decision made and confirmed.

As a consequence, Gerhard devoted much time to aviation during the following months and even hung around one or other air base in the vicinity, so he knew the sound of German planes very well. Hearing the hum of the engines above Meiersberg, he was immediately sure that it must be a British aircraft, probably a bomber on its way home. In 1940 an enemy plane was still a rarity in German airspace. Gerhard rushed outside before all the other inhabitants of Meiersberg. And there an enormous shadow rushed along the wide village road over the rooftops. This flying dinosaur loomed over the village, and was evidently struggling to maintain its altitude. Although the Meiersberg residents knew that their village was not worth a single British bomb and that no danger could come from this monster slogging homewards, they all had a queasy feeling in their stomachs. They stared into the blue evening sky, which was not yet so dark that the contours of the British bomber were not visible, and watched as it took a slight right turn at the end of the village towards the Baltic Sea. When the humming had almost ceased, there was a flash far on the horizon, so far from Meiersberg that that evening nobody set off to investigate the cause. They spoke a few quiet words and wished each other a good night. Only in the morning did a feeling of helplessness creep over everybody when the postman brought news to the village that the British plane had crashed into a farm near Gambin on the Baltic coast and that the unfortunate crew, evidently incapable of controlling their damaged machine any longer, had taken a farming family of four to their deaths alongside themselves. The war had now finally arrived in Western Pomerania.

Gerhard did not waste much time on brooding. He continued his research and was not dissuaded from his purpose of finding out everything about his ancestors even after the 'accident', as the inhabitants of Meiersberg called the bomber crash. And so he quickly came across the name of Gundlach again. The remarkable Gundlach family, he thought to himself, and began to read from the very beginning.

The first church record commenced with a long-winded description of the building of the church and its dedication. It was written by the very hand of Johann Jürgen Gundlach, who had financed the construction of the church from his private means. Later, Gerhard could no longer remember how he had found out the existence of a family association to Gundlach, Gundelach or von Gundlach, which his family, the Ehlerts, had joined at one point. The Gundelachs at any rate had their seat in Großalmerode in Northern Hesse, 33km south of Göttingen. They published family news letters, which are probably still in the possession of the Ehlerts. Herein all kinds of contributions were gathered, sometimes unimportant matters, but also the entire chronicle of Ferdinandshof. One article was most interesting because it reported the history of the Gundlach family in great detail.

It began in Bamberg. The family called themselves Gundloch at that time. The Gundlochs were a respected patrician family who were first mentioned in documents in 1122. For three hundred years they were administrators at the minster and council members. They owned several estates in the village of Oberhaid, 8km north-west of Bamberg. The church there held no right to a preacher, so a priest by the name of Schack from the neighbouring village of Trunstadt held services in Oberhaid. When Oberhaid obtained the right to a preacher, Schack wanted to keep his income from there, although he no longer held services. The payment was withheld and a legal battle commenced in which the bishop of Bamberg found in favour of Schack. This angered the inhabitants of Oberhaid. Heinrich Gundloch, the highest tax-payer, was particularly affected. When Gundloch and Schack met by chance on 22 September 1409 in the Truhending cathedral court of Bamberg, a heated argument took place during which Gundloch flew into such a rage that he stabbed Schack with his dagger.

The perpetrator gave himself up immediately and showed remorse. A court chaired by the bishop of Bamberg was held, and on 30 May 1410 the sentence was pronounced. Heinrich Gundloch was 'mercifully forgiven his crime'. Yet as penance the family was to donate 50lb of wax every year for all eternity, and – very embarrassing – every year Heinrich was to walk barefoot and bareheaded, holding a 2lb wax candle, in front of the church procession around the court of the fortress of Bamberg.

In 1413 even more impositions were made but after the Gundloch family had built another chapel, the chapel of St Katherine in Bamberg, they had had enough. The Gundlochs left Bamberg, but it was still a long time before Albert Ehlert and his sons.

From 1460 onwards there were no longer any Gundlochs in Bamberg. They turned to Hesse, to Großalmerode. There, Heinrich and Kurt Gundloch first appeared in the records in 1461 – the same people who were last mentioned in Bamberg in 1453. However, the spelling of their surname name was altered and Gundloch became Gundlach. This might not have been intentional, but due to the inattentiveness of a scribe.

Großalmerode was the glass making centre of the Holy Roman Empire of the German Nation, as Germany – which was divided into numerous individual territorial sovereignties – was called at that time. The Gundelachs had to adapt to their new environment and learned the glassmaking trade. Due to their leadership qualities, from 1537 onwards they sat without interruption on the board of the glassmaker guild for the next 150 years. Every year on Pentecost Monday all guild masters of the empire had to travel to Großalmerode. In the morning they held session and decided new guild rules. The patron of this meeting was the landgrave (count) of Hesse. In the afternoon an ox was roasted and a public festival was celebrated.

Gerhard read these books for days and could not tear himself away. Deeper and deeper he delved into his family's history and pictured to himself how his ancestors had looked, spoken and propagated, and how they spread across half of Germany.

In the eighth church record he reached the sixteenth century. At its end a new economic system was developed, mercantilism. In order to strengthen the economy, all goods required ought preferably to be produced domestically. With dirigiste interventions in the economy, the absolutist rulers saw to it that as many wares as possible were exported and as few goods as possible were imported. Glass was among the expensive products, so each ruler wanted to have glass works in his own territory. Glassmakers were sought after people, and many princes begged the specialists of Großalmerode to erect a glass works for them.

Thus, the Gundelachs took up the offer of a prince and in 1655 moved to Preetz in Holstein. In 1705 they received an invitation by the Swedish administration in Szczecin to erect a glass works in the region of Ueckermünde Heath. There, on the sandy soil, the best fuel was growing: beech forests as far as the eye could see. Johann Jürgen Gundelach followed this call. He owned several glass works in Mecklenburg and was a master glassmaker, a large-scale entrepreneur. He chose a low hill called the Scharmützel as the location for his home and his production site. Today the church of Ferdinandshof is situated there. Potassium carbonate was needed for the production of glass, and there were already kilns for producing it in the village. Furthermore, Ueckermünde, with its port for shipping the glass ware, was not far away.

On 21 December 1705 a contract was agreed and production commenced two years later. Gundelach arrived with several relatives, who also represented him when absent, and with a labour force for the glass works. Various specialist craftsmen were needed: blowers, stretchers, blow moulders, stokers, workmen, pile hewers and ash drivers. In addition, carters and case makers were employed.

Soon, however, the enterprise was pursued by bad luck: in 1708 a plague ravaging Poland spread to East Prussia and a third of the population died. In 1712 Russian soldiers invaded Western Pomerania in pursuit of Swedish troops and plundered the glass works in its entirety. The family fled abroad – 3km away to neighbouring Mecklenburg. Production stopped for three years, until in 1714 the territory fell to Prussia. The glass works was restored and production resumed. It remained in operation until its closure in 1743.

Gundelach built his house on the Scharmützel, the first in Ferdinandshof, and the church. He brought back some baptismal angels from a trip to Lübeck. Gundelach died in Ueckermünde in 1737 and was buried in his church. Buried next to him was Christoph Ludwig Henrici of Ueckermünde, Royal Notary, True War and Domain Councillor, Bailiff of Königsholland, an administrative district slightly smaller than the later district of Ueckermünde.

Prussia fought under the leadership of the Soldier King Frederick William I in the Great Northern War alongside Russia, Denmark and Saxony against Carl XII of Sweden. In 1715 it received as its prize a part of Western Pomerania stretching from the Oder to the Peene river. The western part, 'Swedish Pomerania', remained under Swedish rule and only became part of Prussia in 1815. Prussia's main focus was the port of Szczecin. Gerhard

Ehlert's homeland thus became Prussian – and it was not long until the founding of Meiersberg.

In December 1747 a hurricane raged across Western Pomerania, causing great havoc on Ueckermünde Heath. Prince Moritz of Dessau, Pomerania's chief civil servant, youngest son of the 'Old Dessauer' (Prince Leopold I of Anhalt-Dessau, 1676–1747, commander of the Prussian–Saxonian army in the Great Northern War), visited the area in the company of the head forester of Western Pomerania, Meier, who lived in Torgelow. After the inspection it was decided to erect several glass works at the edge of the forest in order to process the huge amount of dead wood in a sensible manner.

Ehlert's native village thus owed its origin to a natural disaster. The founding year is given as 1749, since it is first mentioned in writing on 1 February 1749 under the name Meiersberg to honour the aforementioned head forester Meier. It is certain, however, that the construction of the glass works had already begun in 1748. Around 1900 Anna Koppermann opened a general store on these premises. She was Gerhard's great aunt and the wife of Otto Koppermann, the youngest brother of his grandfather, Albert Koppermann. In order to purchase goods for her store, Anna travelled regularly to Szczecin.

After reading this aspect of his family history, Gerhard thought of her as a remarkable, resourceful woman. For Gerhard's great aunt did everything by herself. Her husband had worked in Berlin since 1885 as a mason for the construction of the Reichstag building, together with four other Koppermanns, among them Gerhard's grandfather. This was not the last time that the Ehlert family and their ancestors worked on epoch-making German monuments or took part in epoch-making events.

Great aunt Anna instructed her four children not to dig too deep in the yard, because there might still be relics of the abandoned glass works around in the form of sharp-edged glass. Little Gerhard learned this later from Anna's youngest daughter Wally during one of her visits to Göttingen.

Anna's store changed ownership at some point, but as a little boy Gerhard visited his great aunt frequently. And while reading the church records he recalled once again all the tempting smells that had tickled his senses in Aunt Anna's shop. He remembered the distinctive smells of wooden clogs, cloths, sauerkraut, herring, toy whips for little boys and chewing tobacco, and melancholy seized him and caused him to take pause for many moments.

Eventually he turned the page and read of the glass workers in his family who erected their thatched timber framework cottages in the village. Thatched roofs were a mark of poverty at that time, though today it is probably the most expensive type of roofing. The glass workers had a small holding of 5 hectares on which they could cultivate rye and potatoes, with a meadow providing hay for fodder, three pigs, two cows and chicken. The women were responsible for the farming tasks and the upbringing of their many children. Sometimes the grandparents helped with the domestic chores. Sunday meant a full day's work on the farm almost all year round.

The dead wood of the great hurricane of 1747 had been processed within slightly less than ten years, and the glass works were closed. Most of the workmen remained, since they no longer depended on their primary work but had built up their small holdings and were self-sufficient. For most the yield of the small holdings were not enough to live on, however, and so they had to learn additional trades. As a result, the village of Meiersberg evolved into a craftsmen's settlement. The origin of the glassworkers is not known exactly, but it can be assumed that many came from the south-west of Germany.

The other part of village, dedicated to farming, immediately west of the already existing glass works settlement, was founded in the summer of 1749. The settlement came about on the initiative of the Prussian King Frederick II, who endeavoured to attract settlers to his sparsely populated land in order to balance the losses in human life incurred by his many wars. The farmers in this part of the village came from Mecklenburg and Swedish Pomerania. Their ancestors had moved there for the most part from Schleswig-Holstein in the course of the Eastern Colonisation by the Teutonic Order around 1100. This explains the local Low German dialect, which resembles that spoken in Holstein. Furthermore, many family names here are also common in Schleswig-Holstein. The name of Ehlert occurs frequently, even more so in its plural form Ehlers.

In other villages many settlers came from south-west Germany. The farmers were allocated holdings of 20 hectares and with this size they were full-time farmers. This part of the village was called Schlabrendorff. It was common at that time to name newly founded villages after high Prussian officials of the War and Domain Chambers in Szczecin and Berlin, although they already had other names. For example, the former Hühnersdorf was called Aschersleben after the president of the Chamber Georg Wilhelm von

Aschersleben. Blumenthal, formerly Schale Heide, was named after His Excellency Adam Ludwig von Blumenthal of Berlin, Real Privy Councillor and Finance, War and Engineering Minister. The former Brandhorst received the name of the Privy Councillor and Director of the Chamber Ernst Wilhelm von Schlabrendorff. This practice had already become established in the reign of King Frederick William I, who on the occasion of an inspection trip, renamed four villages after his sons: Ferdinandshof, Friedrichshagen, Wilhelmsburg and Heinrichsweide, formerly Mückenhorst.

Since Schlabrendorff was too jarring to the ears of the dialect-speaking village inhabitants, they turned the name into Schlabberndorf. That sounded slightly derogatory and so they settled on Meiersberg. In church documents, however, the traditional name Schlabrendorff was still in use during the 1930s.

The craftsmen from the original glass works settlement later worked as masons and carpenters, and in brickworks. Many were employed by an iron foundry. In the Ueckermünde district, bog iron ore could be found as a thin layer at a shallow depth, which coloured the pump water brown. In the local dialect this valuable raw material was called the 'red fox' (*de root Voss*). The mining of this iron-rich layer led to the establishment of several iron foundries. After wistfully putting down the twelfth and last church register, Gerhard Ehlert knew that absolutely everything in and around Meiersberg in Western Pomerania was founded on ash – the ash for which the hurricane of 1747 had provided the fodder.

Ehlert wants to summon up Riele's image, but there is no time left, as he needs to concentrate fully on flying. He takes the aircraft in a curve from left to right and vice versa, in order not to offer a straight flight path as a target to the anti-aircraft position below. The pencil in the glass dome dances wildly from side to side.

'Damn it, we need to get out of here, Lieutenant Sir', Schlotter croaks into his microphone. 'Hard right, Lieutenant Sir.'

Now there are crashes high and low. The white puffs left by the grenades from the anti-aircraft cannon when they explode get closer and closer. With a trembling voice, the professor sends off a final radio message to their airfield and reports their last position, although he does not know exactly where they actually are. When he reports being under fire, ground control answers with 'GL. GL. GL.'. Good luck, good luck, good luck! Then one of the two vertical tails receives a first hit, which causes immediate, severe difficulties for Ehlert. The Do 217 can hardly be steered any longer. The pilot uses his entire physical strength. Sweat runs down his forehead into his aviator goggles. And then he instinctively turns on the automatic control. The aircraft takes up a dead straight course, which facilitates targeting for the anti-aircraft position.

The night is markedly bright. There is a full moon and a clear sky. It is 1.15am, the time that will later be entered into the war diary of Luftflotte 2 next to the sentence: radio communication with 'K7+FK' ceases. Their altitude is a mere 80m at this point. Ehlert thinks: 'This is just as well, since the lower we are, the faster we will pass the anti-aircraft positions.' Yet he does not reckon with the Russians. Suddenly the Do 217 receives battery fire from the back. As the Russian soldiers need too much time to target the low-flying German aircraft directly, they simply fire after Ehlert and his comrades – and hit. First the right engine receives a direct hit and catches fire immediately. Then it is as if the plane as a whole is riddled with bullets by a gigantic shotgun. Glass is scattering everywhere, and sharp metal fragments are sailing through the air. Wherever there is fuel – inside the wings, in tubes and pipelines – the plane is ablaze. Leutnant Gerhard Ehlert's Do 217 looks like a comet with a fiery tail.

The men sit inside their plane like Baron Münchhausen on top of his cannonball, which will at some point reach the zenith of its trajectory and then will inexorably crash down to earth. For the Russian gunners on the ground this is a lovely sight, for the German crew a desperate fight for survival. And as if the whole pageant of fire was not enough, a blood-curdling scream penetrates the ears of the men in their burning coffin. The professor has been hit. A piece of shrapnel has ripped open his face and torn away his glasses. Covered in blood, he gasps for air. Burr drops his machine gun and climbs forward to him. He is still screaming for his life, but the screams subside into a death rattle. When Burr finally reaches Unteroffizier Williges, he sees instantly that the boy is already beyond help. The sharp iron fragment of a grenade has severed the jugular. The professor is bleeding from a gaping wound, is no longer able to talk, whimpers and gasps, and stares imploringly at his comrade, Aerial Gunner Willi Burr, with his uninjured eye. Help me, the eye tries to say. Behind a veil of blood and tears, the professor sees Burr's face as he leans over him and in desperation presses a ridiculously small dressing onto his jugular. From the expression of his comrade the professor realises that he is lost, that he will die, here and now, above this goddamn front line inside this goddamn aircraft, which will soon cease to exist.

Burr cannot pretend, cannot comfort his fatally wounded comrade, cannot give him a look of hope. Even the slightest smile hurts. He does not want to be a liar during Williges' last minutes.

'Our Father in heaven, hallowed be your name.' Burr is praying into his microphone and the professor, from whom the grenade has torn away the headphones and microphone, does not need to hear it, as he can read it from Burr's lips. Then the dying man has lost so much blood that he faints. He will not experience the actual crash. And Williges' mother will once again hear the fugue, just as with the death of her husband.

Burr is crying desperately, and the two others inside the craft know what has happened without the gunner having to tell them. The pencil inside the glass dome under the seat of Observer Hanns Schlotter comes to a halt for a moment, as if it wishes to salute the dead.

If Ehlert had not been shaken to the marrow by Karl-Heinz Williges' death scream and Willi Burr's crying, he would have tried to calmly move the aircraft out of the line of fire. From his position as pilot, at the very front of the Do 217, he can only see the right engine burning. Not too bad, he thinks. For a few minutes he does not realise what a dangerous situation the entire aircraft and its crew are in. As long as we are flying, we do not need to worry, he tries to convince himself. Then, however, he fixes his eyes on the altimeter and speed indicator. Suddenly he realises that the plane is on the verge of crashing. At best there will be an uncontrolled crash landing. The chances of survival would be near zero for all inside the aircraft, as the young pilot knows only too well. For a twin-engine plane like theirs there is no suitable spot for a pancake landing at night and on land. If there is a field, the plane will overturn at 300km per hour. The whole machine will come apart, in Ehlert's reckoning. He imagines the even worse scenario of the aircraft crashing into the forest or against a building at the same speed. The pilot foresees that nobody will survive either crash option, and panic rises up inside him. How long until the event? Ten, thirty or even a hundred seconds? In any case, only seconds.

Gerhard lets his short life pass in front of his inner eye and thinks of his father. Always his father. It is thanks to him that Gerhard became a soldier. It is due to him that he is now sitting inside this death trap. His father, Albert, born in 1894, whose ancestors had spent their lives working their farm, was slender and tall and had dark hair. From an early age he had learned to play the violin and baritone horn from a 'town piper' (a musician in the employ of a town council) in Ueckermünde, with whom he also lodged. During this time the old Europe prepared for its first great war.

As millions of others, Albert Ehlert became a soldier in 1913 in Szczecin, after finishing his apprenticeship. He entered the war at the beginning as a volunteer. For a short period he was deployed to Russia, then to France for the remainder of the war. There he experienced the horror of the battles at the Somme, at Verdun, at Winterberg and near Reims. His hair turned grey. His wife and sons noticed this during his short leave from the front in 1916, yet they did not ask any questions. Albert held back and remained silent. Apart from one dramatic incident, a dispatch ride during which his horse was fatally hit by nine bullets, though he remained unharmed, he had nothing to tell of the war to his sons. What is more, he kept his participation in daily life to a minimum. It was as if he had unlearned civilian life. Nevertheless, the leave was over much sooner than his sons would have liked.

Albert Ehlert was never wounded, at least he never told of an injury. Yet his silence aroused the curiosity of his sons. The silence that had fallen over an entire generation of world war veterans would be the germ for the next conflict, the worst global conflagration of all times. His sons did not know any better when they were driven into the next slaughterhouse by Nazi propaganda.

All this comes to the young pilot's mind. It is as if he has pondered this for hours, when the aircraft touches the ground for half a second, then ascends slightly again. In his mind Gerhard says a calm goodbye to his girlfriend, Riele. She had given him a talisman, a little elephant made of ivory, which he carries in the watch pocket of his trousers day in and day out. He takes it in his right hand, clenches his fist around it as if for protection and imagines how difficult it will be for the Russians to open his dead fist. If he dies now, he wants to hold something of Riele. If he is to die he wishes to take it along with him.

The three men still alive inside the mortally wounded aircraft wait for the big bang, a crash with a tree or a house. Each of them clings to their seat. At the front the pilot Gerhard Ehlert, below him inside the glass dome the observer, Oberfeldwebel Hanns Schlotter from Frankfurt am Main. Behind them the aerial gunner, Willi Burr from Heidenheim. The latter cannot avert his gaze from the dead professor, whose corpse looks like a strange red bundle of bones, skin and flight suit.

Ehlert thinks to himself that it will be dark after the crash and silent, overwhelmingly silent. Then they hear a loud scarping, crashing and rattling.

A jolt seizes the aircraft, a terrible jolt that rips the bottom away from under them. No, not the bottom, but the glass dome below the pilot – there where the pencil ceases to dance and where Schlotter dies at this second. First both legs are torn from the Oberfeldwebel, then the front part of the dome crushes the remainder of the lifeless body and drags it to the back. The crushed Schlotter and the shattered Do 217 no longer belong together. The tall Oberfeldwebel with the keen eyes and the crooked nose falls onto a green meadow wet with hoar frost. Hanni Schlotter and her two sons, Fritz, three years old, and Max, just one year old, will never see their husband and father again. A glass dome has become his coffin, and nobody will ever be able to place a cross onto his grave because there is no grave.

Meanwhile, the two others are still fighting for their lives. The torso of the shattered aircraft provides protection. The plane, or rather what is left of it, slides across the meadow like a sleigh ride during the Bavarian winter. Yet for the survivors the seconds of gliding turn into an eternity of terror.

And then? Then nothing happens, simply nothing. Silence falls. Only the low crackling of the fires can be heard. The large glass dome has not only broken away below the pilot, but in front of him, too. This saves Ehlert's life. If it had not broken away, he would not have been able to leave the plane and would probably have burnt to death. The pilot is shocked and thunderstruck when the Do 217 comes to a halt. He has the presence of mind to climb to the front and out of the aircraft. He is entirely unharmed. His first thought is rather stupid: Gerhard, now you have to go home on foot. The second thought, however, is quite clear: let's scram. Away from the nearly empty tanks with the highly explosive gas mixture and away from the eight flash bombs that are still on board and which might explode any moment. Ehlert runs for his life. After a few seconds he meets Burr, who is about to remove his parachute. Then the two run away from the crash site. After 200m they throw themselves on the ground. At any moment the entire craft will go off with a loud bang. Yet again, nothing happens. The machine continues to burn silently and steadily. The two dare to prowl around the burning plane. They look for Schlotter, quietly call his name, but he can no longer hear them. Schlotter's remains are scattered across the crash site. It is just as well that these two do not know this. Their courage might have left them. As it is they briefly confer with one another. They have to leave this site before the Russians arrive. After a few minutes, only ashes remain of the Do 217.

3

Swamps

After a few hundred metres of breathless flight the Leutnant and the Unteroffizier consider themselves to be safe. They take a short breather, leaning against a tall tree that offers them shelter in the bright moonlight. Ehlert's skull throbs with exertion. Burr's burnt skin begins to smart, and his heart is racing madly. For the first time since their initial hit by the anti-air-craft battery over the Russian front line they take a few minutes to appraise their situation. Burr examines his body by touch, especially the parts burn-ing like fire – hands, cheeks, part of his ribcage that was not entirely covered by his flight suit. The palpable heat radiating off his skin notwithstanding, everything feels damp and uneven. Fear arises and takes hold of him. Why did I have to get soaked by the damn aviation fuel, Burr asks himself and in the same moment feels ashamed because he has to think of the professor whose dead body they could not recover from the burning aircraft.

While Burr examines his injuries, the pilot next to him thinks of a thou-sand matters. Where exactly were they when their plane got hit? How far is it to the front line? Burr does not know anything more than I do, Ehlert thinks to himself. There is no need to drive him crazy with my questions. And then Ehlert reruns their flight path in his head, thinks long and hard where the crash site has to be located, and finally, after ten long minutes, lets his gunner in on the result of his musings. 'I estimate 60 kilometres. We will need three nights,' Ehlert whispers.

'And then?' asks Burr and feels his own desperation like a cold shower trickling down his skin. 'How will we get to our lines without being captured by the Russians or shot by our own people, Leutnant Sir?'

'All in good time', Ehlert whispers, stretches his limbs and slowly straight-ens himself by clinging to the tree. Burr follows his lead. He feels dizzy. Ehlert sees his comrade swaying. 'Let me have a look, Burr. How bad is it?'

'It's okay. Not worth mentioning, Leutnant Sir.'

By the light of the moon Ehlert inspects Burr's burns. And indeed: 'As far as I can see in this light, Burr, everything is of a lovely red colour and covered in splendid blisters. That's wonderful. It would be bad if your skin had turned black. It will hurt a little. By the time you get married everything will have healed again!'

The word 'married' causes both of them to wince. They face each other silently, until Ehlert regains his composure and gives Burr a sign that they will rest for a few more minutes. Now the Unteroffizier has time to think of his home, his Linda, her blonde hair, which she tucks behind her ears. The one lock of hair that keeps falling into her face. Her radiant smile. And Burr knows that she could have anybody in Mergelstetten. 'But I only want to be with you, Willi, you know that', she had whispered into his ear, and laughed when he had uttered his concerns at the end of his last leave. Her laughter now causes him doubts. Would she still want me if she saw me now, this thought crosses his mind. And his doubts are more painful right now than his burning flesh.

Ehlert knows no doubts. He knows that Riele will stick with him no matter what. They are simply made for each other. No one could be more suited to each other. She was eighteen years old, he twenty, when he noticed her for the first time. This was in Kolberg (Kolobrzeg), the old fortress city at the Baltic Sea that will suffer a terrible fate towards the end of the war. Ehlert had been stationed there a few days earlier, at the neighbouring airfield in Bodenhagen (Bagicz). From this airfield the first fighter planes had taken off in late summer 1939 to bomb Polish towns and cities. Now that the young pilot had finished war college in Werder near Potsdam, he had been deployed there with another sixty aviators. It was February 1942. While soldiers were already dying before Moscow, the young pilots in Kolberg enjoyed life to the full. When off duty they lounged around in pubs, enjoyed long walks along the Baltic Sea, visited concerts at the Ufa Palace (a cinema named after the Universum Film AG, a major German film company producing and distributing motion pictures from 1917 through to the end of the Nazi era) or allowed themselves to be invited to illustrious parties. It was a merry, carefree life in the midst of war.

One afternoon, Ehlert was cycling from the airfield to the town and he saw her walking along the road, muffled in a coat, with a red scarf wrapped around her head. Even from far away her delicate figure exercised an incredible allure on him. Over the next few days, their paths crossed again and again, the young Leutnant and the schoolgirl. Every eye contact confirmed Ehlert in his view that he would not be able to forget this woman. He made a great effort to concentrate on his training, but his thoughts strayed to her with increasing frequency. By now he knew her name and which school she was attending. Pilots are masters of reconnaissance. Gabriele – Riele – Müller. Their glances met time and again, and eventually he caught a first smile. Yet it took weeks, even months, until they exchanged their first words.

Again the Leutnant was travelling by bike when he passed Riele in the company of a school friend. Again he was unfocussed, and as a result he began to swerve back and forth on his bike – so clumsily that in order not to fall he had to stop abruptly not long after passing the two young ladies. The girls giggled, and finally Gerhard had a pretence to talk to them. Bluntly he chided them that they should not laugh at a German officer because of a little mishap. Yet in the same instant he realised how he had scared the young ladies with his bluntness. He followed his remark with an apologetic smile and engaged the two in a trivial conversation, of which Riele and he became more and more the focal point. Riele's girlfriend realised that she was superfluous and left them under a pretext.

Then Riele and Gerhard continued to talk for a little while, and he prolonged their meeting until he found the courage to invite Riele to the cinema. She accepted without the slightest hesitation and from this moment on they were inseparable. They visited each other, and after two months Gerhard introduced his Riele to his family. It was the beginning of a great love that will outlast all horrors – even the horror Burr and Ehlert have just survived: the downing of their aircraft, the professor's death, the fact that they did not find Schlotter near the burning plane, and the situation they are in, in the heart of enemy territory without provisions. A wild animal, which passes the tree they are leaning against with a snort and which they cannot discern clearly despite the moonlight, startles them from their thoughts. Linda and Riele have to wait.

Again it is Burr who wants to know what will happen next, whether it even makes sense to attempt reaching their own lines. And again it is Ehlert who calms him down. 'Have no fear, Burr. In this area here, there are not only Russian partisans, but also some from the Ukraine. These are on our side and have already helped several shot down flight crews across the front line.'

Ehlert puts great conviction into his voice, even though he himself does not know yet how they will be able to contact these friendly partisans, the more so as they plan to travel only by night and do not speak a single word of Ukrainian.

Ehlert is so annoyed with his own stupid idea that he jumps up. 'Come on, Burr, we have to go!'

Then they begin their long trudge through the Pripyat Marshes. Usually one envisions a quagmire when hearing the word 'marsh', boggy ground into which one sinks with every step. The Pripyat Marshes situated between the rivers Bug and Dnieper are entirely different. For thousands of square miles, forests and meadows are submerged in centimetres-deep water. At the bottom the ground is firm. It is as if God has emptied out a huge bucket and forgotten to mop it up. The Marshes are a flooded area ratherthan a real swamp. The cause is the very low gradient of the water courses crossing the region and because the southern tributaries thaw much earlier than the northern ones. Ehlert is surprised that his brain is already functioning again and that he itches to impart his knowledge of Europe's largest swampland to Burr. The latter would most likely once more consider him a know-it-all.

Ehlert refrains from doing so, also because he has to increasingly contend with pests that descend in their thousands onto the two soldiers: mosquitoes. 'Miserable creepy-crawlies. They will devour such little twerps as us whole, Leutnant Sir', Burr mutters to himself, still joking.

In reality, however, the two will realise over the course of the next few days that these tiny critters are not harmless at all. From innumerable spots, even through the cloth of their uniforms, they suck the blood from the men's bodies, and their bites become inflamed, pus-filled blisters. Soon Ehlert and Burr look like they have the bubonic plague. Before long they will furthermore discover that Burr has some severe, painful burns. Yet at this moment he does not feel any pain. The adrenalin pumping through his veins, released by the crash, paralyses his nerves.

Ehlert and Burr make good progress at first. They march north. Ehlert does not have to consult his wrist compass once. They do not need a compass, since the night is starlit and the Pole Star guides their route. Williges' death still affects them both, but they are of good cheer, nevertheless. They are free. That is the most important matter. For now they are still free. They slink across wide swaths of grass under the moonlight, interspersed with wooded areas in darkness. They try to make no racket so that no Russian will take notice of them. If the area is slightly hilly, they find a couple of dry spots on which they can rest for a few minutes.

They plan to march until the first light of dawn and then to hide themselves. But then a village suddenly appears in front of them, illuminated by the moon. They emerged from dense undergrowth right in the middle of the village high street. They fling themselves into the ditch and hold their breath.

'Rats! I hope nobody has seen us. We have to give it a wide berth in my opinion, Leutnant Sir', Burr whispers and receives a nod from his superior.

Just as they try to hide again in the undergrowth, a figure walks up the road. Don't move now, Ehlert thinks and presses his face into the dirt. Burr does the same. They hear the heavy steps of a man. The boots thud ponderously onto the dust. He must be a giant. Then he comes to a halt, just 10m away from their puny ditch. Ehlert is already envisaging what will happen next. His imagination rides a roller coaster. Russian shouts, lights are turned on, soldiers erupt from the houses, aim at the two German air force soldiers and fire. At that moment the giant lights a cigarette – just in time before Ehlert's fancy completely runs away with him. The smell of Machorka is in the air, the strong Russian tobacco. The two minutes, during which the man hastily smokes his stub, turn into an eternity. If he only turned his gaze a little to the left, in the moonlight enhanced by the glow of his cigarette, he could not help but discover the two men in their ditch.

Burr smells the giant's breath, who now comes closer to them step by step. The giant mutters to himself and chuckles. Russian soliloquies are not much different from German ones, Ehlert thinks to himself. The story inside the giant's head requires so much concentration that he does not even notice the two German soldiers, when he steps on Ehlert's left hand. The pilot grits his teeth. He is lucky, because the ground below his fingers yields slightly. The pain is bearable, he thinks. Yet he has not reckoned with the giant. The Russian turns on his heel and presses Ehlert's fingers into the ground. Now it is really difficult not to scream. Ehlert bites down onto his lower lip and tastes blood in his mouth. Then Burr and he are able to breathe again. The giant flicks the stub into their ditch, turns around and strolls back to the village. Step by step he moves away.

'What a stroke of luck, Burr', the Leutnant whispers.

Burr answers: 'We ought to make ourselves scarce.'

They crawl on all fours out of the ditch and back into the undergrowth, where they pause to catch a breath. Then they give a wide berth to the village. Their direction is towards the north; that is where they suspect the front line to be. And thus they creep slowly and silently all through the night.

Awfully slowly. So slowly that they would need three weeks to cover 60km. Yet their recent experience near the village has killed their appetite for bold action.

At some point dawn is approaching. Ehlert and his gunner look for a hiding place. A copse on a hill seems suitable to them. It shelters them from view, and most of all it is dry. As the first rays of the morning sun already provide some warmth, they can finally take off their wet clothes and dry them. During the night they had to wade through several brooks and even to swim through a small river. Ehlert's boots, his breeches with the suede applications and his thick white polo-neck jumper are steaming in the sunshine. He hangs his khaki-coloured flight suit over a tree branch, not too high that it will be noticed. The Leutnant's jacket bears his insignia and badge so he is recognisable as a soldier despite the unusual uniform. According to regulations, he carries his aviator ID with his name and rank, nothing more. Unfortunately Burr also carries his pay book, which Ehlert now shreds to pieces and throws away. 'In case the Russians catch us', he reasons.

Before they rest, in their half-naked state the two forage for food in the immediate vicinity of their provisional camp. Apart from a few berries that they cannot identify and thus do not eat they do not find anything edible. Burr is so thirsty that he take a large gulp from a puddle. Then they lie down and look up through the trees into the blue sky. Burr starts to snore softly and rhythmically. And suddenly Ehlert becomes very calm. A strange feeling steals over him. Only for this one day throughout his entire life will he feel this particular, strong emotion: an exalted, strong feeling of being completely free. This peculiar emotion can only arise if one knows that one is wanted and hunted, but has not been caught yet and is still free.

In this strange mood Ehlert thinks of his father, wonders how the latter became the way he is, and ponders the reasons why he got involved in this damned war without due consideration and scrutiny. He sees little white clouds drifting across the sky, which in his imagination almost form the silhouette of his father. Then suddenly there are those clouds again left behind by anti-aircraft grenades when they explode near planes – near *his* plane.

Gerhard pulls himself together and makes a great effort to push the drama over the anti-aircraft position to the back of his mind, the crash, the death of his radio operator Williges whom they called the professor. Ehlert wants to recall his father as precisely as possible, recalling everything he knows about him to the last detail, on the one hand to keep his mind occupied and on the other hand to find answers. Why is he the way he is? Why is he lying under some trees in enemy territory and not next to Riele? What has his father got to do with it?

Everything! At that time fathers have everything to do with the lives of their sons. For Albert Ehlert is one man among millions who let themselves be driven into the First World War, the first great global conflagration. Then, in 1914, the war was widely welcomed. A few years later it is exactly like the one Ehlert is stuck in now: just really miserable, Ehlert thinks to himself. And again the image of the dead professor rises before his mind's eye without him being able to blank out the horrific pictures of the latter's grave injuries to his throat and face.

Suddenly the elated feeling of the so far successful escape vanishes. He feels cast down. And again his father is with him, his father with his tall, slender figure and the full dark hair. He is of an athletic type. Although a born soldier, he initially studied to be a musician, learning from Ueckermünde's town piper.

Gerhard Ehlert does not know in this moment of deceptive calm under the blue Russian sky that he and Burr have only a little time left to enjoy their freedom. He ought to be more wary, as the forest scent is mixed with another, intense smell, that of freshly mowed grass. Where meadows are mowed, farmers are not far away. Russian farmers. He and his Unteroffizier had planned to only march during complete darkness, but the searing summer sun and their restlessness do not let them rest after just a brief nap. They give in to the irresistible urge to go on.

At first everything goes as planned. In the early dusk they leave the elevated copse providing shelter – much too early for darkness to give them cover. They are torn between tension, relief, impatience and mourning. Their steps become quicker, the trails they take become wider tracks, the tracks turn into paths. Faster and faster they want to go. They are almost running now and abandon all caution. Suddenly they are standing on a wide, dusty road. And then it is already too late. A boy comes towards them, driving cattle before him.

'Let's go,' Burr hisses and intends for them to hide in the undergrowth. But Ehlert has quickly regained his composure. 'It's just a little boy.' And now he approaches the boy. The cowherd, perhaps twelve years of age, halts. Ehlert smiles at him and holds his palms up. Look, we do not have weapons. This is a lie because he has salvaged his pistol from the Do 217. Then the pilot starts to gesticulate with his hands and gropes for the few words of

Russian he has been taught during the last weeks of his training. 'Soldiers, partisans nearby?'

The boy understands and shakes his head. Or does he understand? Or is he even lying? The two will learn this soon enough. The boy leaves them standing there and continues on his way with his cattle. He clearly looks uncomfortable, even though he pretends to be friendly and calm. Ehlert and Burr stare after him, their mouths open, as if they cannot fathom the lack of concern with which the boy resumes his task, although he just came upon two German soldiers.

Is it courage or indifference driving the boy? Even when he is some distance away he does not walk faster. He could start running now and the two Germans would probably not be able to catch up with him. Yet the boy walks slowly besides his cows as if nothing has happened.

Ehlert and Burr sit down on the side of the dusty road. Their throats are hurting with thirst. Their bellies grumble. It is still twilight and their encounter with the cowherd should have been warning enough to the German Leutnant and his Unteroffizier But the calm exuding from the boy with whom they exchanged gestures, the deceptive safety and indifference communicated by him, makes the two of them even more incautious. They remain on the road, at first crouched low and ready to jump, then walking upright.

After a few hundred metres they reach the edge of a clearing and give a jerk. Over there, slightly more than a stone's throw away, are three log cabins at the edge of the forest, almost hidden below the first lines of trees. Nevertheless, their silhouettes are clearly visible. There is the smell of freshly chopped wood in the air, and smoke. The scent of something frying, too. That clouds the minds of the German soldiers, and only a few metres away from the log cabins they realise that they have just passed some women digging something from the ground of the little field in front of the cabins.

Dinner, potatoes, Burr thinks, and Ehlert quickly turns on his own axis. Securing the perimeter, as he learned at officers' school. The women seem timid and apprehensive when they spot the two Germans. They whisper with each other, and Ehlert is only able to discern their head scarves. At this distance it is already too dark to see their faces. They merely discern the head scarves, talking to each other in front of the dark log cabins that smell of food, rest and peace. Ehlert yearns to sit down on one of the benches in front of the cabins and to make small talk with the women – about the weather, God and the universe.

There it is again, this peaceful feeling inside of him, this contentment. He almost smiles. Yet then one of the women approaches him directly. Too late he realises that she is holding a rake in one of her hands. He suppresses his smile and straightens himself. She is supposed to realise that he is ready, that he will not be massacred by a woman on a field. Not he! And not Burr, whom he hears breathing at his back, either. A few metres in front of the two soldiers the woman comes to a halt. And again Ehlert only perceives the head scarf. Is it red? Is it Riele's? Riele's head scarf? Damn it! Pull yourself together, Gerhard, he curses himself.

The woman with the red head scarf greets him in a language he has never heard before and which has nothing in common with the Russian he knows to some extent. Ehlert answers '*dobre djin*', good day, just as he was taught. And then the woman with the scarf finally answers him in Russian. This is almost a relief, even though he only understands a few words in this language.

Then Ehlert spits out the usual questions: 'Soldiers, partisans nearby?' She answers the Germans with an apparent no and says much more. With many gestures and words, the woman talks insistently to the two men, and Ehlert joins in. Somewhere he has read that as long as you talk to your enemies, they will not kill you. After minutes of back and forth one thing is clear: the women are evidently on their own, and the men all dead. Ehlert believes them, wants to believe them all too willingly, and Burr makes no move to be cautious, either. It is war, what worse can happen to us than death, thinks Burr, who is actually no longer able to think at all as he is much too hot despite the coolness of the twilight.

Ehlert gets the woman with the red head scarf to lead them into one of the cabins. The other women walk slowly to the two remaining huts, dust off their shoes and vanish behind creaking doors.

Bread and milk! For the first time in his life the Leutnant eats dry bread. He chews it hungrily and it tastes delicious. After a few bites and a large gulp of milk, Ehlert looks around for his Unteroffizier Butt does not want to eat anything. He is wax pale and shivering. 'Gosh! Burr, what is the matter?'

Only now Ehlert perceives the burn blisters on the Unteroffizier's face, which have grown into huge yellow lumps during the last few hours. Every spot on Burr's body not covered by his uniform during the crash shows such blisters, which look like pus-filled lumps with air under a thin dome. Ehlert looks more closely at his gunner and forces him to drink some milk at least. Burr obeys. As usual, he obeys. Then he collapses onto a bench, trembling. 'I believe, Leutnant Sir, I cannot go on for a while.'

'It will all be fine', the young pilot says and is immediately ashamed of his secret thoughts: Damn it, what next? Why could Burr not take better care of himself? That is arrant nonsense, of course. Who can take care of themselves during a crash landing?

While Burr stretches out on the bench and Ehlert takes care of the piece of bread provided by the woman with the red scarf, the latter has left the cabin without a word. Again Ehlert ought to be suspicious, again he ought to urge caution, but he chews and drinks and drinks and chews and looks at the trembling Burr. At the last moment he looks through the window and notices a silhouette flitting past. Ehlert leaps to the door and sees the boy running down the road.

'Damn it. Something is wrong here,' the Leutnant hisses to the room at large, and Burr slowly sits up. 'We have to leave. Immediately!' While Ehlert splashes his face with water from a basin on top of a dresser, adjusts his boots and his dusty, ragged uniform, Burr has taken up position at the window. Silently and with a sigh on his lips he turns to his pilot. 'Leutnant Sir, Leutnant Sir, we are lost.'

Instinctively, Ehlert reaches for his pistol stuck in his boot leg, loads it with a cautious click and cocks the weapon. With a single look Burr drives home that this will make not the slightest difference. He shakes his head, just a few millimetres left and right, and then lowers it. Ehlert knows what this means. They do not stand the slightest chance. A loaded and cocked pistol means certain death for them both.

Ehlert lowers the pistol, engages the safety and puts it down on the table, almost tenderly. He takes a crumb of bread between his teeth, resumes his chewing and waits. As yet, the enemy is only a shadow outside the cabin. Thus far he is not real, not tangible. And yet the two men inside this log cabin at the edge of the Pripyat Marshes in the middle of the Soviet Union know that the end of their freedom is standing outside the door.

It takes an endless thirty seconds, then a man opens the door with a single, violent kick. For the first time in their lives Burr and Ehlert stand eye to eye with a Red Army soldier. The young soldier looks clean and well-groomed, he is wearing a brand new uniform with a pressed appearance about it. He aims his rifle at the two Germans, and the bayonet fixed to it gleams in the light of the candles on the table in the cabin.

He is afraid. Ehlert perceives this in his eyes and he can smell it, too. The young Russian did not know what to expect inside the hut. He had to reckon on being shot down by the two Germans when entering the house. Yet no blood will flow this evening. The Russian does not let the pistol on the table out of his sight for even a moment, then he swipes it into one of the cabin's corners with his bayonet.

'*Dawei, dawei*', he says to the two Germans. Now he seems entirely calm and relaxed. He is the victor in this fight that never happened. Ehlert will later recall not the rifle, but the uniform, this clean, pressed earthy-brown shirt, the polished boots only faintly dusty, the gleaming steel helmet. Whoever has such clean soldiers cannot lose the war.

Ehlert and Burr step out of the hut without raising their hands. At that moment, twenty, no thirty, Red Army soldiers form a semicircle around them and load their rifles. Ehlert realises that Burr has saved his life. One shot from his pistol and the entire troop would have opened fire on them and the log cabin. He does not know what weighs more in this second: the relief to be still alive or the fear of what will happen now.

4

Captured

Capture means beatings, kicks to their groins, to their heads. Wild shouting, jabs with the bayonet, blows with the rifle butt to their faces until their skullcaps are ringing, being stripped naked – all rumours Ehlert and Burr have heard about the 'Bolshevik subhumans', as the Nazi propaganda calls the Red Army soldiers. The first minutes of being captured take their imagination on a roller coaster ride.

Ehlert breaks out in a cold sweat, Burr's similar reaction could also be caused by his fever. Both expect the worst. Yet nothing happens. They will not be able to recount anything dramatic to their children and grandchildren later if they survive this damned war, nothing but that they are searched by a few clean, calm soldiers in earthy-brown, freshly pressed uniforms. It is the first time that they are searched thoroughly, by four or five soldiers at once. Everybody wants to pilfer something.

'Watch, watch?' the Russians ask. Without resistance Burr surrenders his watch – what else could he have done? Then three men tug at the leather strap around Ehlert's right arm until it tears off. The disappointment is visible on the Russians' faces when they realise that this is only the compass. Another soldier with Mongolian features, who has held back until now, searches all the pockets of the two Germans once more in a leisurely manner, after the others have left off of them, and is indeed lucky. Ehlert will never forget the expression on the Mongol's face when he picks a pencil from one of the pockets. With a happy, joyous look he turns away from the two aviators, clutching his treasure. The Russian commander of the operation, a captain, takes Ehlert's pistol as his prize and without glancing at it tucks it nonchalantly into his belt – a trophy befitting his rank, his expression seems to say. Then the Russians gather their things. Most of them shoulder their rifles, and the Mongol points with a machine gun down the road: '*Dawei!*'

The long road into captivity begins for the two German aviators with a trip by truck along the road on which they moved without caution towards the front line, towards home. Now the truck carries them in the opposite direction. Burr, still in much pain, stares blankly at the floor of the truck. Ehlert looks at their Russian guards, one after the other. How foreign they are, how strange their features seem. And still, their laughter is like ours, Ehlert thinks to himself with peculiar calmness. He looks at the dentures made of steel many Russians display. Even the incisors are formed from steel. Everything smells new and strange, the fuel burnt by the truck, the air they travel through, the uniforms of the Russians, who are jarred on the truck bed just like their German prisoners. Often one of the Russians comes very close to Ehlert during these jolts so that the latter perceives his scent quite intensely.

When they are driving through forested areas it is pitch black on the truck, but among the meadows and fields the last light of dusk is gleaming. The Germans see the foreign tanks and artillery pieces at the side of the road. They see – for them something completely unheard of – armed women in the same uniforms as the male Russian soldiers. Everything, really everything is strange, and Ehlert asks himself what he is supposed to do in this country, what he is doing on this truck and why he ever went to Russia in the first place where everything is just so strange. Only the scent is already familiar to the German officer, it is the smell of Machorka, the tobacco smoked by all Russians.

After a few kilometres the prisoner transport stops in front of a wooden house, which evidently holds a command post. All around it camp fires are burning, tents are visible, and Ehlert is reminded of a youth camp of the boy scouts. It is just like in peacetime, if one could overlook the brand new weapons, the ammunition boxes, the artillery pieces and the armoured vehicles.

The Russians jump down from their truck, loudly greet other Russians, laugh, cuss and smirk. They would have almost forgotten the two Germans, if the captain did not bellow a few orders and then vanish. Two Russians take Ehlert and Burr into the wooden house, which is illuminated brightly. They are led into a room with just a table and a single chair. Nothing is hung on the walls, nothing superfluous is standing around. A petroleum lamp lights the room.

The Russians quickly make their intentions clear. The prisoners have to strip until naked. Now the actual frisking begins. Their two guards take everything off the Germans, even their underwear, which is no longer white as befits a German Leutnant and an Unteroffizier. Rather it is as field grey as the army uniforms. Ehlert smiles while making the connection with the trench warriors. Now we are not better off than they are, us air force toffs, he thinks to himself. Yet his smile turns rigid in the next moment when one of the Russians discovers the tiny tuck inside the hem of Ehlert's trousers and the item within.

'Talisman?' one of the soldiers asks, and Ehlert nods in the hope that the Russian would show a little compassion, sympathy for the importance of such a personal effect. Yet Riele's ivory elephant disappears into the trouser pocket of the Russian soldier. It is lost forever and for the first time Ehlert feels depressed. Anxiety overwhelms him with such force that he could actually burst into tears. He never learned crying either from his mother or father; he will have to learn it now.

After the Russians have searched everything thoroughly, the Germans receive their clothes back. Then they are simply left standing in the brightly illuminated room. The Russians disappear, but Ehlert notices that one of them positions himself outside the door.

It might be midnight when they are finally led outside. One Russian prods the two Germans into a foxhole with his rifle butt, their camp for the night. In spite of their dejection or because of it, Ehlert and Burr fall asleep immediately. The night is balmy, the foxhole dry and there is a scent of freshly cut grass and warm stones in the air. Their first night in captivity could be worse.

They are awoken late the next morning, when the sun is already well above the horizon. 'Dawei, dawei!' A soldier leads them through the camp. At that moment the two Germans realise why this war can no longer be won. There is a bustle as if inside a beehive. That which they already considered threatening from the bird's-eye view of their reconnaissance plane months ago has an overwhelming effect on the ground. Hundreds of perfectly outfitted soldiers, masses of military equipment, ammunition tents filled to their roofs, stock pots full to the brim, Red Army soldiers in marching formation, Red Army soldiers in small groups, long queues of Red Army soldiers, Red Army soldiers as far as the eye can see. And among them the two Germans and a single soldier, who pulls on his cigarette and shows them their way with a single glance. One against two. Even half a guard would have sufficed, for where could the two captives flee amidst this Red Army sea?

Slowly Ehlert and Burr stumble through a wooded area. Before them spreads a wide dirt track, and behind them walks the single Red Army soldier, singing loudly, continually smoking a cigarette. He carries a hip flask from which he takes a careful sip every few minutes as if it was the last vodka on offer during this war. The trees become denser, the track narrows and the Russian becomes quieter. Ehlert observes him sucking the last drop from his hip flask and his expression is darkening. The Russian stomps silently and grudgingly after his two prisoners.

Ehlert develops disquieting thoughts. What if the Russian has finally enough of leading the Germans through this wilderness? What if the Red Army soldier stumbles or makes a false move with his machine gun? Perhaps, so Ehlert reasons with himself, perhaps they ought to simply overpower this fellow with his narrow eyes and even narrower lips, this disagreeable vodka fiend. Here the forest is so dense and they are already so far away from the Russian army camp that nobody would notice this surprise attack. And as if Burr had the same thought in this very same moment, he looks at Ehlert with a meaningful expression. Yet the two have not reckoned with the Russian vodka devil. The latter seems to suspect that the two Germans are up to some mischief, curses loudly and shouts something that Ehlert and Burr do not understand even after its third repetition. Then the Russian cocks his machine gun – an announcement universally understood by every soldier regardless of their mother tongue.

Only a few minutes pass, then the three of them are suddenly standing in a huge clearing. The two captives suspect that their flight would have ended here at the latest. From this section of the front there is no way out, this has become evident to Ehlert and Burr. Here the Russians are everywhere. With open mouths they observe the bustle in front of them. They are standing at the edge of a gigantic airfield with hundreds of planes, though now there is not much activity. A few trainee pilots are practising circling approaches with their biplanes.

This is no different from our airfields, Ehlert thinks. It seems half an eternity ago to him that he himself was a trainee pilot, in 1941 at Werder near Potsdam. It seems a thousand years since he sat in a biplane, in those days at the aerial warfare school in Werder. Now he feels as old as the hills among all these eighteen-year-old Russians just learning to fly. And yet his recollections of his training have not faded, primarily because he spent exciting months at the school. He will never forget the day in June when he narrowly escaped death because he had forgotten to pull a tiny lever. He had already done thirty take-offs and landings in a Bücker 131 Jungmann (a 1930s basic training aircraft) with the flight instructor and thirty solo flights with this biplane, which was as solidly built as none other of its era. You can get 180km/h out of this aircraft, and he always went full throttle as soon as he was out of sight of the flight instructor. Or he throttled back when flying above the girls presenting themselves in their bathing suits in the vicinity of the flight school attended by the trainee pilots. Then the young cadets sometimes went down to a low altitude and took a good look at these young ladies.

By now Ehlert knew exactly what he needed to do to keep the aircraft on course. He knew that he had to continually steer slightly to the right because the spin of the propeller always pulled the biplane slightly to the left. Ehlert was familiar with the aircraft's behaviour while turning left or right, during roll and during inverted flight. Acrobatic flight was a component of their training early on, because their instructors wanted their students to all but merge with their aircraft.

At the end of their initial training they were all excellent pilots, so fine that they became reckless. During this phase most of the accidents happened, because the young men overestimated their skills or simply switched off their brains. Ehlert was among the best, and so it was no surprise that he was supposed to fly one of the five biplanes when his training group of six instructors and thirty trainees was transferred from Werder to Borkheide.

Four of the five pilots assigned had already taken off, and his other comrades were travelling by bus. Only Ehlert and the head instructor – a strict, po-faced officer – a few mechanics and a driver were still at the airfield in Werder. The head instructor signalled with his flag that the runway was clear, and Ehlert took his foot of the brake. The biplane zoomed up into the sky, and the young pilot handled everything as taught. The propeller cut the air and the engine was running smoothly. He soon reached the intended altitude of 150m and gained more and more speed. The air was whistling around the pilot's ears.

One second later he no longer trusted his ears. A strange noise came from the front. The engine stuttered, the propeller stood still. Horizontally. The aircraft stalled. For an experienced pilot this was no problem. You simply turn to gliding. And even Ehlert knew, despite the early stage in his aviator career, what to do. He immediately took a wide turn in order to return to the airfield. This, however, cost him so much of his limited altitude that the biplane almost touched the first tree tops after just a few metres. There was no point in tugging at the joystick or in cursing. Ehlert's aircraft plummeted rapidly and hurtled towards a forested area. The pilot tried everything to pull the biplane in a different direction. Too late. With a loud splintering noise, the lower wing shaved off a tree top and within the next twenty seconds chopped off one branch after another during its plummet to the ground. It snapped small trees and splintered the wood into small pieces. Finally, the engine pierced the forest soil. The propeller, undamaged, was still horizontal. Then everything fell silent. Ehlert saw and heard nothing. Then he smelled something. A wonderful scent of resin reached his nose, and then he became aware that he was still alive. He had been very lucky. He was almost uninjured.

At the same time a rescue team left the airfield. The remains of the aircraft ought to be salvaged and brought back as soon as possible, the dead pilot recovered. Yet their astonishment was great when the men came upon Ehlert. The crash pilot was sitting on top of his parachute next to the wreckage and was in high spirits. Ehlert's good mood, which was only dampened by the fact that the propeller had remained intact and thus could not be carried off as a trophy, infuriated the head instructor. He already suspected what had happened. One look at the petrol cock of the plane and it was evident: Ehlert had been sloppy. Not a drop of fuel had reached the engine because the pilot had forgotten to open the petrol cock. That meant two days of light arrest on bread and water and a three-month cut to his aviator allowance; that quickly wiped the smirk off Ehlert's face.

There is another reason, however, why he will never forget this day. It was 22 June 1941. Loudspeakers all over Germany sounded a melody from Franz Liszt's *Les Préludes* and the voice of the Minister for Propaganda, Joseph Goebbels, announced: 'Soldiers on the Eastern Front! At this instant a deployment of troops is taking place which the world has not yet seen.' The attack on the Soviet Union had begun.

Three years had passed since then, three years during which Ehlert became a soldier and went to war, but during which he had never had occasion to internalise the war in the manner in which the infantry soldier, the tank crewman, the pioneer and the medic do. These men he now sees in the Russian army camps, marching eastwards in drawn-out columns, their hands clasped behind their heads, their faces unrecognisable under the smudge of dust, sweat and dirt, in tattered and discoloured uniforms, with bloody bandages around their limbs, their naked swollen feet wrapped in a few rags. All this depresses him badly, and Burr next to him suffers likewise. At the sight of the German prisoners they feel like crying. This here is the real war, the war of the ground warriors that panned out so badly for the Wehrmacht in Stalingrad in January 1943 and has since just got worse and worse. This is completely different from the bird's-eye view where face-to-face fights do not exist. In the air you do not have to expect to be hit between the eyes by a Russian bullet at every minute of your life or to be torn apart by a grenade.

If Ehlert is honest, he has to admit that he did not even carry a real weapon on board his Do 217 apart from his own pistol and Burr's machine gun. We were shooting with a flashlight and camera, that is like war with cotton buds, he mutters to himself and spits out laughter. Then he thinks of the dead professor and of the missing Schlotter. He still does not know that the latter's remains cling to the burnt metal of his wrecked aircraft in the Pripyat Marches.

The Russian guard puts his hand on Ehlert's shoulder and wakes him with a shake. They are standing before the biplanes of the Red Army trainee pilots and it feels a little bit like home. Burr and Ehlert take a seat next to the young aviators. Immediately a conversation starts – with hands and feet, with snatches of Russian and German. The Red Army soldiers touch the flight suits of the two German aviators again and again. 'Substitute, substitute,' they jeer disparagingly. Their propaganda has made them believe that Germany is on the rocks and their clothing is made from substandard material. And indeed, when Ehlert looks down on himself, he realises that even the German uniforms are now inferior to the Russian ones. The enemy has received a million pairs of boots from the United States. The allies beyond the big pond deliver trucks, ammunition, tanks and uniform cloth – an inexhaustible reservoir of war material that is shipped to the port of Murmansk on the Barents Sea and from there is often thrown directly into battle. While the cities and factories are burning in Germany, the Red Army has an abundantly stocked general store directly in their backyard.

Soon an officer of slight build, a major, joins the two German aviators. He is supposed to accompany them during the coming week. Then two tall Red Army soldiers report loudly to the major. One of them hands him a written order, which does not bode well because as a result Burr is lead away by the two hulks. Burr and Ehlert have grown close during the last few days. Their crash, their rescue from the burning aircraft, their initially successful flight, Burr's burns – of which both of them took care, their capture and march through the forest, hunger and thirst, the elation of the hunted of not being caught yet – all that has bound them together, the posh Leutnant and the sometimes ungainly Unteroffizier. And even though Ehlert's upbringing and his training as an officer spoke against it, indeed his entire nature struggled against it, he nearly offered Burr the informal address '*Du*' (you). Somehow or other, however, the right moment did not present itself. And thus it is a military farewell the two are exchanging. Burr smartly salutes his superior: 'I'm signing off, Leutnant Sir', he shouts at his pilot. And the two face each other like two boys who have done something stupid on the playground and are now apologising to each other.

Then Burr is led away. The Unteroffizier has to climb inside a box mounted to the lower wing of one of the biplanes. A typical Russian construction, simple but effective. The box is normally used for the transport of the wounded. Burr lets himself be bundled up without complaint – what else is he supposed to do? The last glimpse Ehlert has of him are the burn blisters on his face and his dark blond mop of hair. Then the lid is closed.

Now it is his turn. He has to squeeze into the back seat of another biplane together with the major. The pilot takes the front seat and now pulls a lever and cranks something here, something there. A simple aircraft, easy to start, the German pilot thinks. He is watching his Russian colleague closely. Before Ehlert knows it, the biplane and its three passengers has taken off and is flying towards the south-east. Shortly thereafter it starts to rain, and visibility turns poor. In addition, twilight is settling slowly, which causes the pilot to interrupt the prisoner transport after an hour's flight. He lands on a wide dirt track and taxies his aircraft under a tree. The major and Ehlert are jolly glad to leave the plane and stretch their limbs. A night's rest under the open sky is the order of the moment. The Russians are so nonchalant that they do not take even the slightest security measures. They make themselves comfortable under the tree, chat with each other, laugh and cuss without paying any attention to their prisoner.

The major – he wears thick glasses with a huge frame – and the pilot are both not very brawny. Furthermore, they are not heavily armed, on the contrary! If the major was not wearing a pistol on his belt, the two would actually be unarmed. Ehlert considers his situation briefly and comes up with a daring plan. His body tenses in its seated position and he gets ready to jump up. His brain is working feverishly and he notices adrenalin slowly pumping through his veins. His face reddens – he hopes the Russians will not notice it in the twilight. Like a film, the ideal scenario plays out in his mind's eye: quick as lightning he deals the two Russians uppercuts, they are knocked over dazed and confused, and he mounts the aircraft, starts the engine, takes off and lands at his home airfield among loud cheers. A splendid fantasy! But what will happen if he is not able to incapacitate the major with his first blow? What if the pilot has a pistol hidden somewhere? What if the engine does not start instantly? Ehlert has never dealt an uppercut before. He therefore does not know if he has enough strength to cause a brief fainting spell. There are so many unknowns! And yet, if he could muster some courage now and act swiftly it could be his chance to flee, perhaps the last chance to get home quickly.

And as if the Russians are able to visualise Ehlert's internal struggle, they are both grinning from ear to ear. The major opens the holster with the weapon, takes it out carefully and loads it. Then he screws up his face, his smile vanishes in a flash and he takes on a threatening posture. He aims his pistol at Ehlert. 'Bang!'

The major and the pilot nearly die of laughter when they see the rigid expression on their captive's face and realise what fright they caused with their little joke. Throughout the night the two Red Army soldiers take turns. One of them stays awake at all times, and Ehlert is no longer thinking of flight.

The next morning, after a short flight the three land in front of a large command post at the edge of a town. The major and the pilot hand over their prisoner to two soldiers on guard. Before leaving they say a proper farewell to the German, clap him on his shoulder and repeat their little joke: 'Bang!' If the two were not such friendly fellows Ehlert would have been incandescent with rage. As it is, he patiently endures their making fun of him, returns their friendly smiles, nods his head and grins. Then the ceremony is over, and one of the guards pushes the German pilot into a small room on the ground floor close to the entrance to the command post.

The room is immersed in semi-darkness. Only sparse light trickles through a small latticed window far above. Ehlert notices immediately that he is not alone. Back in one corner of the room a figure crouches on top of a bare steel berth. 'Leutnant Ehlert, Luftflotte 2, Army Group Centre.' He has not finished his brief report yet when the figure jumps up and snaps to attention: 'Unteroffizier Wilhelm Burr, also Luftflotte 2, Leutnant Sir', the figure cheerily reports back. 'Gosh, Burr, old chap, that we are meeting again! How was the flight inside the box?' 'Splendid, Leutnant Sir, I nearly fell asleep because I was so comfy. And yours?' 'Not quite as comfortable, but it was okay.' Burr does not need to know that he lost his courage when there was a chance to flee and that the Russians made fun of him.

During the next few hours the two prisoners talk little. They are tired to their bones. And what could they tell each other anyway? After all, they have experienced everything together. Now for the first time they encounter fleas. They are itching everywhere, and the three stings close together – typical for the evil tiny creepy-crawlies – can be found all over their bodies. 'Even the damned mosquitoes were more bearable than this,' Burr curses. The fleas become their most faithful companions.

During the next few days they meet a young man in civilian clothes who is staying at the command post. Ehlert makes friends with this Russian pilot, of whom it never becomes clear why he is staying here. Ehlert learns that he was shot down over German territory and parachuted from his aircraft. Polish people gave him civilian clothes and brought him across the front line. As a reward for his brave return, he received one month's leave in Moscow, his home city.

From the first moment of their encounter, the two men do not view each other as enemies but kindred spirits. They belong to the internationally bonded guild of aviators. The pilot lends Ehlert his 'comb', a 4cm middle fragment of a real comb, and his 'mirror', a small shard. If the two Germans are pestered or insulted by some Russian soldier, the aviator rebukes him. The Russian calls Ehlert '*pichota*' with a smirk. This means infantry soldier and is, of course, quite an insult for a fly boy. In general, the following days pass quite casually at the command post.

As Ehlert is not allowed a razor, the officer of the guards gives him a daily shave, a twenty-five-year-old officer with blond hair and a central European appearance, but a native of Siberia. 'I will leave the moustache. You can shave it off when you are back in Germany. Then you have a goal to look forward to,' the Russian says with a smile. Ehlert will keep to this notion. He knows that from this moment onward his moustache is an outward sign of his not being home. He does not know yet, however, that he will wear this moustache for quite some time.

Every evening the news is read aloud – also in German. A female interpreter – a young Russian woman from Leningrad who had studied in Hamburg before the war – takes on this task, a little haltingly, but with a great passion. While she is translating, Ehlert perceives that she wishes to make the language of Goethe and Schiller her own. In the twilight the

German phrases are accompanied by mournful folk songs played by a Red Army soldier on his accordion.

It is as if time stands still at this command post where Ehlert and Burr are held captive. It is as if the war never existed. The days pass and nothing happens. Nothing again, the German pilot thinks. He survived the crash, he was saved during his capture by the fact that Burr persuaded him to put away his pistol, and he made peace with his maker in the forest near the Russian airfield, when the path narrowed and his guard stopped singing. Nothing and nothing again. It is as if he – and perhaps also Burr – is being protected by an invisible force, as if a sheltering hand is being held over them. When he thinks of their crash alone, terror washes over him. Exactly six! He can think of six lucky breaks he has had without hesitation.

On six occasions during just a few minutes everything had to go well so that they were able to survive the crash. It began with the fact that Ehlert instinctively turned on the automatic control, which kept the plane on a straight course, after he was no longer able to keep the rudder steady after the first hit by the anti-aircraft battery. When the right engine suddenly caught fire and malfunctioned, the plane would otherwise have taken a sharp right turn, which the battered aircraft would probably not have survived. It would have side-slipped and hit the ground like a sack of potatoes. The automatic control prevented that.

Then their angle of descent. Before touchdown this had been so shallow that touching the ground did not cause the plane to turn over. This correlates materially to the fact that the Do 217 is a shoulder-wing plane. This type of air-craft maintains an extremely stable flight attitude, even with stalling engines.

The third guardian angel intervened at the moment and place of Ehlert and Burr's crash landing. The pilot was no longer able to influence the land-ing. It was mere coincidence, pure luck, that the aircraft touched down on very level terrain without an obstacle between a forested area and a village.

Then, Ehlert continues to ponder, the fourth stroke of luck: the cockpit, the glass dome, broke off shortly before the plane came to a halt, so that Burr and he were able to climb out of the aircraft. They would probably have burnt to death if the dome had remained attached to the plane.

The fifth lucky break: he and Burr had an advantage in that their seats were at the aircraft's left side. There they were placed on top of a 50cm-high ped-estal shielding them from severe injuries, injuries that had killed Schlotter, which Ehlert still did not know.

And finally the last lucky circumstance: the decision to approach the Russian women, to visit the village. It meant their capture in the end, but what would have happened, so was Ehlert thinking now, if they had encountered some Russians during their march through the nocturnal forest, Red Army soldiers or even partisans? And he is certain by now that this would have been as sure as night follows day. In the darkness the Russians would have given short shrift. All this crosses Ehlert's mind. And because he can hardly believe his luck, his mouth hangs wide open during this consideration. And Burr, who is watching him from the other end of the table, knows exactly what the Leutnant is thinking in this moment and how he feels.

The musical evenings at the command post slowly take on an orchestral scale. More and more Russians attend the command post in the evening. More and more instruments and voices can be heard. Still, that does not change the sad undertone of the songs. There is a depth to the Russians' character, a peculiar ponderousness that drags Burr and Ehlert down into a dark hell, in which they have to think about the war and their enemies who treat them so well. So these are those 'subhumans', as they were portrayed by National Socialist propaganda in such a brutal black-and-white manner in its ideological fervour. These are the bloodthirsty, barbarian, uncivilised Bolsheviks. These people with their wonderfully melancholic songs of an immense country with endless rivers and infinite coastlines, with sempiternal winters at the Polar sea and searing summers in the Kalmuk Steppe, are supposed to be an inferior human race. The subhumans are playing trumpet and violin here. Ehlert is as sick as a dog at the thought of all the lies told about the Russians at home.

During a halting conversation with the interpreter Irina one evening, he lets slip the remark that he can play the violin, too. Immediately he is proffered an old instrument, which he seizes with reverence and at which he stares as if it was the most valuable thing in the world. Here, in the middle of Russia, he the fascist pilot is given such an instrument.

'Strauß, Strauß,' the horde of Russians is chanting in the large common room of the command post. So Ehlert plays a waltz by Strauß. When he has finished and lowers the violin, silence prevails. One could hear a pin drop. The young commander of the guard detail, the Siberian, is the first to applaud slowly and quietly. Then the others join in, and it ends with cheers that would have moved Ehlert to tears, if he had learned to cry.

In those days Burr is treated attentively for his burns by a good-natured, plump Russian nurse from Odessa. She seems like an immovable figure from a Baroque painting. Yet when she performs her slow-motion-like movements, she shows her efficiency in all that she does. She mothers the German prisoner like a brooding hen, salves his wounds, and even washes his feet. Burr bears her attentions with pleasure.

When the occasion arises, Ehlert asks her for a towel and soap and receives her answer: '*Saftra budit* – tomorrow it will be!' So tomorrow. Only much later Burr and Ehlert will learn that '*saftra budit*' is a Russian phrase without any real meaning that is heard on all occasions, at all times of the day and in every emotional state of the speaker. 'We are living in the land of the Saftrades and Budites,' will become a popular saying with the German captives.

Days and nights pass, and the Germans gradually forget that they actually have no place here in Russia. They receive three meals a day, are shaved and can wash themselves – even though they do not have soap or a towel. In the evenings Russian news is read aloud to them from the newspaper, and they play music with their guards while drinking copious amounts of vodka. Then they learn of the attempt on Hitler's life by Colonel Count Stauffenberg and of the failed coup by the 20 July conspirators. They have discussions with their Russian comrades on loyalty and obedience, as if they were educated together at an officers' school. For both sides it is a matter of course not to stick the knife into their fatherland, even if one does not like the political leadership. And the Germans in particular get excited and gush about the traditional concepts of generations: honour, fatherland, duty.

'If the fatherland is in danger, you have to fight for your people, regardless of who is king at that time, and regardless of how he is treating his subjects,' Burr states categorically. And Ehlert ponders. What has more weight? Blind obedience or high moral standards? From which red line onwards does tyrannicide become an obligation? These are questions that keep him occupied until late into the night.

The following morning, doom approaches in the form of an American jeep driven by a corporal to chauffeur a Russian major and a lieutenant; the lieutenant in the front, the short thin major in the back. With a squeal of the brakes, the vehicle stops in front of the command post. It is a busy, nervous squeal that startles all inside the building – whether captive or not. It is long lasting like a siren, an alarm boding ill.

The major wears a spanking uniform, and his cape of heavy cloth swishes audibly through the air as he jumps out of the jeep. The lieutenant wears wire-framed glasses like the professor, whose remains most likely are still lying inside the charred aircraft on a meadow near Sarny.

Then inside the building the word '*Nemez*' is heard. Burr and Ehlert know immediately that this means them. '*Nemez*' means German. For the first time for days the two prisoners are split up and locked into separate rooms on the ground floor of the command post. From this minute onward nothing remains as it was. Tchaikovsky and Strauß have had it. Now a different tone prevails, and the major is promptly trying it out on Ehlert.

For his interrogation, the German pilot is brought into a small room with armchairs and coffee tables. The short, wiry major with his sly face, reminding Ehlert somehow of an animal – which animal he cannot bring to his mind that instant – offers him a cigarette. Ehlert's first mistake: he does not smoke and hence is in the major's eyes not only suspicious but unlikeable.

The major and his lieutenant, an interpreter probably in his mid-twenties, from this moment become the constant companions of the German captives. The main dramatis personae from now on stay the same: Burr, Ehlert, the major and the lieutenant. The background actors change daily. Every morning a new specialist of the Red Army is wheeled in from somewhere to grill the Germans.

The Russians want to know everything about the different areas of German reconnaissance aviation. How do the pilots fly by night? Why is their blind landing successful? How do German pilots react to the appearance of night fighters, to interaction with anti-aircraft positions, to contact with spotlights? How does photography with a flashlight work? What are the most important technical advances of German radio communication?

Ehlert has to pay very close attention to how much he should divulge to the enemy. Enemy? Yes, they are back again. The Russian sitting opposite of him acts like an enemy. He is questioned with guile and deviousness. They probe and exert subtle pressure. Ehlert knows that this Russian major and his lieutenant will tighten the thumbscrews more and more. He is resolved to explain nothing of the technique and training of blind landing, no matter what.

Blind landing is as if you are driving at 300km/h in a Mercedes Silver Arrow on the motorway – only while blindfolded. This is the explanation Ehlert had heard from Burr shortly before they ran their Do 217 into the ground.

Blind landing is a technique that at that time has been mastered best by the Germans. Blind landing is the supreme discipline of aviation at a time when there exists only rudimentary radar, no ground radar and much less an auto-pilot. Blind landing can only be managed by hearing and with a lot of discipline. If the Russians knew how it worked they could reduce every German airfield to rubble by night. They could simply bomb blindly instead of landing blind.

Blind landing works like this: from the ground a radio beacon sends a sustained sound to the plane in the air. The pilot hears a sonorous, even hum if he is on course. If he deviates too far left he hears an interrupted hum, protracted and interspersed with short, sharp intervals. If the plane deviates right of the course, the intervals are longer and the hum shorter and more distinct. To stay on course horizontally is relatively easy. That is common knowledge among the German pilots. It becomes more difficult when land-ing, because then you have to also factor in the vertical dimension. A few hundred metres away from the runway with an infernal machine of 3,000 horsepower under your bum, showing 300km/h on its speedometer – and then nothing but darkest night or dense fog.

Now signals for high and low are added to the sounds for left and right. Again you have to differentiate between humming and bleeping sounds. And then there are the outer markers that inform the pilot on the distance to the runway and what needs to be done in which situation.

One of the first outer markers signals the man at the joystick that he has to extend the landing gear. Too high, too low, too far left, too far right – it bleeps and hums wildly inside the headphones. It is easier to concentrate on one's hearing, because the eyes do not send signals to the brain – and yet the nerves are at breaking point during each landing.

Ehlert learned blind landing, flying without ground visibility, in January and February 1943 at the Blind Flight School 3 in Prague – in those days when the 6th Army froze and bled to death at Stalingrad. Four weeks of hard training at the joystick – day and night – were their schedule – and not for one moment did the young pilots think of the defeat looming in the east.

Ehlert saw only a little of the beautiful city of Prague. He managed to visit the castle district and Wenceslas Square. Once he went to the opera. Ehlert was accommodated in an apartment building confiscated by the Wehrmacht. He shared a room with another pilot. His roommate was none other than Hans-Werner Große, the future world-famous glider pilot with fifty world records to his name. Yet this would have nearly not come about. For the two trainee pilots almost lost their lives due to carelessness – and that on the ground and without enemy contact.

The rooms were heated by tiled stoves. Since neither Ehlert nor Große had experience with this kind of stove, they made a crucial mistake: they closed off the stove door and pipe to the outside in order not to lose any warmth. Thereby both of them failed to notice that the coals had not yet burnt down completely, and they feel asleep. The stove started to give off clouds of pungent smoke, and if Große had not woken up because of a coughing fit, the two of them would have suffocated due to carbon monoxide poisoning. They managed to drag themselves from their room just in time and save themselves. Nevertheless, they had to pay for their carelessness, as they had to stay in the field hospital for days and were almost unable to graduate from the blind flight school. At any rate they had to make up for lost time. In the end both of them passed and proved themselves in the most difficult of aviation disciplines.

Blind flight means visibility of zero to 50m at full speed. The Russians do not fly in such conditions. They remain grounded if visibility is less than 500m.

'In such conditions our crews take off their parachutes and smoke a cigarette out of boredom,' Ehlert thinks to himself and cannot suppress a grin, until a heavy kick is landed on his chair. A Russian colonel is dissatisfied because he sees the German pilot lounging comfortably during the interrogation. He shouts at the other officers that the *Nemez* must stand during their inter-views. Ehlert does not understand immediately; only when the interpreter's boot meets his chair does he realise what is meant. So the German officer stands up. From now on he will remain standing for three hours, three hours during which the Russians sit in their armchairs and smoke Machorka, until the small interrogation room looks like a runway during fog.

Time and again, the colonel tries to intimidate the young German officer with his loud, piercing voice. Some threats he spits out so rapidly one after another that the lieutenant cannot keep up with their interpretation. Ehlert feels bit by bit how his thigh bones are boring into his hip. He notices the tension in his sinews and muscles. He tries not to sway or tremble. This could be interpreted as weakness. A German officer does not tremble, that was hammered into him during his training.

His eyes are watering from the cigarette smoke, his mouth feels dry and his tongue is sticking to its roof. In front of him, on the table with the three

Russian officers behind it, an earthenware jar is placed. What might be its contents, Ehlert wonders so as to distract himself. Again and again the colonel shouts at him, and again and again the interpreter translates quietly: 'At which frequency do your radio beacons transmit at which time? What are the code words for the individual night flying groups? Where are those deployed right now?'

Questions, questions, questions, which gradually dissolve Ehlert's brain. And yet he manages to concentrate so far that he gives the same answer again and again: 'Leutnant Ehlert, Luftflotte 6, 2nd Long-Range Reconnaissance Group.' He tenses his body and snaps to attention. 'I repeat: Leutnant Gerhard Ehlert, Luftflotte 6, 2nd Long-Range Reconnaissance Group.'

He coughs under his breath. Shortly before the muscles of his right thigh start to spasm violently, Ehlert feels the unbearable tension from his knee to his hip. It nearly tears him apart, but he does not move a single millimetre. 'Not yet, Gerhard. Not yet!' he encourages himself. And he is lucky. At some point the colonel has had enough of hearing the same answers again and again. He puts out his cigarette stub and leaves the room, muttering to himself. Ehlert guesses that this was a curse.

Lieutenant and major stand up simultaneously, shake out their weary bones, grin, listen for noises in the corridor where the colonel's steps slowly fade away, and begin to laugh raucously. 'Sit down,' the interpreter tells Ehlert, and the latter enjoys the wooden chair as if it was a princely throne. The interrogation is at an end, and Ehlert slowly realises what the future might hold for him. Casually the interpreter tells him in a quiet manner that he has been to Germany. He had seen how the workers were living there. 'They are all dwelling in foxholes.' The two Russians laugh sneeringly.

Yet Ehlert knows instantly that neither of them has ever been in Germany. He does not answer, but he commits the interpreter's spiteful lie to his memory forever. He will need the lie later, the lie about the foxholes in which the German workers allegedly live. More than that: in all his thoughts in the coming weeks and months this ridiculous lie by the Russian lieutenant will play a crucial role. For now, Ehlert only has a vague premonition.

The days are getting shorter now, not only because the Russian winter is approaching, but also since the intervals between the interrogations become shorter as well. Ehlert has not seen Burr for days. Sometimes he hears his curses in the corridor, sometimes he believes that he hears him shouting. Burr shouts back if he is shouted at by the Russians during his interrogation.

Then, however, one night Burr's shouts fall silent. Nothing can be heard at all. Ehlert falls into a restless sleep. He does not need to be woken in the morning for the next interrogation. This time it is a lieutenant colonel who joins his two guards, whose appearance each day is spick and span.

Ehlert knows immediately that he is facing a new calibre of interview. The smiles have vanished from the major's and lieutenant's faces. The lieutenant colonel slowly and carefully takes off his gloves and puts them on the table. Then he unbuckles his belt and places it – including his pistol – gently next to the gloves. He whispers with the guards and it takes an eternity until he attends to Ehlert, who once again has been standing for a while.

The lieutenant colonel turns to the interpreter and says something in Russian in a low voice. The interview commences, but this time the questions are of an entirely different nature. 'Where are your parents living? Do you how many aerial attacks are flown on Germany each day? What do you think of Hitler?'

'Leutnant Gerhard Ehlert, Luftflotte 6, 2nd Long-Range Reconnaissance Group.' He clicks his heels slightly. 'Yes indeed, Leutnant Gerhard Ehlert, Luftflotte 6, 2nd Long-Range Reconnaissance Group.'

He tenses his body and snaps to attention. 'I repeat: Leutnant Gerhard Ehlert, Luftflotte 6, 2nd Long-Range Reconnaissance Group.'

He is sweating. The lieutenant colonel's eyes never leave Gerhard Ehlert, and as if at a given secret sign their eyes meet, those of the German pilot and the Russian political officer – he wears red stars on his sleeves – both look at the table and the pistol in its holster. For the first time since the crash, Ehlert feels something like fear. For now it is only a tiny niggle in his mind and seems rather unfounded, too. Then, however, the Russian stands up from his armchair, seizes the holster, pulls out a weapon resembling an American colt and jabs the Nagant (a seven-shot, gas-seal revolver made by Belgian industrialist Léon Nagant for the Russian Empire) hard into Ehlert's chest.

Again, without turning around the lieutenant colonel quietly says something to the interpreter, who translates nervously: 'We are not happy with your statements. You have until tomorrow to reconsider.' Ehlert is stricken by terror, and this terror does not go away when the interpreter leads him back to his room and turns the key in the lock behind himself. It does not pass when Ehlert is lying on his back on his berth with his eyes wide open all night. No, for the first time he now feels real terror, feels at his captors' mercy and helpless. How is he to know if the Russian is only bluffing or if he is serious? Apart from a few exceptions, the interrogations had actually been rather like conversations among colleagues, but the Russian lieutenant colonel has put an end to this now. This will never happen again, not during a single interrogation of the dozens still to come. The tone has changed and so also Ehlert's sense of his own captivity. The more he refuses to divulge matters concerning his personal life or concerning professional secrets, the harsher the tone and the more the noose tightens around his neck.

At that moment on top of his berth inside the command post, Ehlert does not have enough spit left to swallow. His head hurts and his heart is hammering. He does not sleep a wink the entire night. Time and again he recalls the Nagant on his chest. He senses the weapon's cold, smooth iron on his ribs, sees in his mind's eye the spiv of a lieutenant colonel with his greased down hair standing opposite him and slowly pulling the trigger. What would it feel like, the bullet penetrating his chest cavity? What is the pain like? Would the bullet tear through his heart or only hit his lung? Ehlert sees blood trickling from his mouth, sees himself fighting for air and screaming silently and inwardly. Then he leaps up from his berth, drenched in sweat and trembling. The lieutenant colonel is just bluffing, he concocts a new truth for himself, and he curls up on his berth in a foetal position.

The nights outside are already cool. Ehlert is sweating and freezing at the same time. He thinks of Riele at home and sees a light. His surroundings become warmer, and the smile playing around his lips nearly does not hurt. Nearly. Yet reality is stronger. He thinks of a saying he has read somewhere: 'To stand once before inexorability where no mother is looking for us and where no wife is crossing our path. Where only reality reigns, cruel and great.'

And this here, at this command post, at the edge of this town, this here is hence reality. Reality in which everything might be over tomorrow. He feels like crying. And then he falls into a light, superficial sleep after all, from which he is eventually woken early in the morning by the blond Siberian, his Russian fellow pilot whom he has not seen for days.

'*Dawei!*' The Russian stands in the door frame and gestures to the German pilot that he should get up. '*Dawei!*' Ehlert looks into the face of the young Russian, who just a few days ago gave him a shave and compelled him to keep his moustache. 'So that you have a goal and can draw a line under this chapter once you are back home again.'

The young Russian's words still ring in Ehlert's ears. Can he sense a smile? Or is there perhaps an expression on the pilot's face that might point to his impending doom?

Ehlert looks the man squarely in the face as if he wants to read it. Yet the Russian appears tired, and his features are blank and bland – like the pages of an unwritten book. Suddenly Ehlert has the notion that the young Russian pilot has no longer anything left to say to him but '*dawei*'. Ehlert drags himself up and slowly follows the Siberian leading him into the interview room. And then? Then nothing happens – again. Simply nothing. No lieutenant colonel, no Nagant, no bullet, no major, no interpreter. Nothing. *Nitchevo*. Nothing. Only a mug of steaming tea placed on the table in front of him, which the Russian offers him with a wave of his hand.

Ehlert drinks and burns his tongue. He would never let his pain show in front of the Russian. Therefore he slowly swallows the much too hot liquid. At home he would most likely cuss, but here he almost has to laugh out loud with joy despite the pain, because in the same moment he is gulping down the hot tea he hears the Siberian's words. 'The interrogation is finished,' the Russian says serenely and wonders whether the German is glad to hear it.

Of course, Ehlert is glad. And how! He wants to embrace his fellow pilot. No Nagant on his chest any more. No reconsideration until tomorrow any more. No interrogation anymore at this god-forsaken command post where he thought he would die. The Russian pilot seems like a blond angel to Ehlert – and yet will disappoint him terribly the very same day.

Yet first the German officer undergoes quite a few formalities. Marching orders are drawn up. It is obvious: the command post here is history. They will continue on, both of them. For suddenly there is Burr again. His face is swollen and his upper lip cut. He has trouble speaking. Evidently, the Russians have treated the German Unteroffizier less decently than the German officer. Yet Ehlert can see in Burr's eyes that they could not beat anything out of him. 'It's alright, Leutnant Sir', the gunner mumbles to his pilot.

Then the Germans receive a proper farewell. Here for the first time they experience the other side of Russian captivity. Outside the command post Ehlert and Burr are greeted by a guard soldier with a machine pistol at the ready. Just as the little contingent is about to set off, the Siberian asks Ehlert inside again. Of course, the German pilot obeys. He will soon learn the meaning of war: there is no friendship among enemies.

The Russian pilot orders the German to take off his boots and hands him a pair of shoes without laces in return. Although the Russian is visibly embarrassed by this setting, that does not change the fact that he exchanges his own poor shoes for Ehlert's tiptop boots. And Burr experiences the same outside. Only he is even more unlucky. He receives a couple of tattered felt shoes for his boots.

'They clearly noticed that our clothes are evidently still quite good and no "substitute"', murmurs Burr when he sees his Leutnant in his lace-less shoes and looks down on himself.

The guard takes the two German captives to a railway station. They have barely arrived when a menacing crowd closes in upon Ehlert and his gunner. At first they only stare at the two. No smile reaches the Germans, no sympathetic or even pitying glance. Ehlert looks around and realises at once what happened in this little town with this railway station. Rubble is scattered everywhere. None of the buildings around the tracks are undamaged. Given the devastation, many must have died.

At the same moment that Ehlert wants to quietly inform his gunner of his discovery, a tiny elderly woman presses forward from the crowd encircling the two German aviators. She points with her walking stick to Ehlert and Burr and shouts: '*Tu Bombider, da, da?*' A murmur goes through the crowd, from which a puny man with a much too large pistol at his belt emerges. With halting but clearly intelligible German, he shouts into the aviators' faces: 'You and you, Hitler swine!' He proudly taps his chest. 'I partisan! Father, mother, brother, sister, you murdered them all. Do you have father, mother, brother, sister?' he harshly demands of Ehlert. 'You will never see those again. When we have finally reached Germany, we will wade through German blood, just like you Hitler swine were swimming in French champagne.' This hate-filled sentence pierces the German officer's soul, and Ehlert senses how the storm might look that they, the Germans, have sown three years ago with their invasion of the Soviet Union.

The Russian guard, who has apparently realised that he is lugging around valuable prisoners, puts an end to this horrific episode at the bombed-out station. With an unmistakable gesture underlined by his machine pistol, he drives the crowd apart. Sullenly and with curses on their lips they trot off, not without firing malignant glances at the Germans first.

Only now do Ehlert and Burr realise the full extent of the destruction that was evidently caused some days earlier by one of the last German bombing raids in this section of the front. Ehlert is amazed that their terribly tattered air fleet was capable of this at all. His amazement grows even more when suddenly their view opens up onto the whole railway station. Endless freight trains with tanks and artillery as far as the eye can see. Some carriages display chalk inscriptions: 'To Berlin!'. Neatly lettered and in German so that the Red Army's arch enemies are able to read them.

At this moment Ehlert has to think of the First World War, of slogans such as '*Jeder Schuss ein Russ*' (every shot a Russian] or '*Jeder Stoß ein Franzos*' (every jab a Frenchman). It is strange that this flashes through his mind right now. He wonders about himself and he is amazed by what he sees at this railway station somewhere in Russia: Russian soldiers in a euphoric mood. Laughing, almost jubilant as they wave at the civilians.

'I don't like this at all, Leutnant Sir. That here is like back home after the French campaign', Burr murmurs.

'I am afraid, Burr, that they have every reason to be like this. Since Stalingrad there has not been much going on with us. But keep quiet about this, Burr. Otherwise we will end up on the gallows through showing defeatism', Ehlert grins, and his gunner answers his grin broadly.

After all, how could they be punished for not believing in a final victory here in the middle of Russia? Long-range reconnaissance aviators like them have not believed in victory for a long time. Too many tanks, too many artillery pieces, and too many Red Army soldiers have had to be noted down on their tally sheets during the recent months. The war is lost. Yet the Leutnant and his Unteroffizier have not just known since this day at the railway station near Baranovichi.

And while the Russian soldiers roll past singing, Ehlert thinks of his school years. He remembers how time and again he picked up the *Dierecke School Atlas for Institutions of Higher Education* and flipped through it so often and for such a long time that many of the maps were virtually committed photographically to his memory. He thinks of the declaration of war by Britain and immediately pictures the British Empire: Canada, large parts of Africa, India, Australia and many other, smaller regions, then the large merchant fleet and navy capable of transporting everything required to Britain. He knew immediately that the close ties to the United States ought not to be discounted. They would support Britain at once through supplies, just as Germany constantly bought materials from other countries. Two minutes later the schoolboy Gerhard Ehlert said to himself: 'We will lose this war.'

What he did not know about at that time was Hitler's mania regarding living space (*Lebensraum*) in the east, which meant war against the Soviet Union. A war on two fronts! Madness, Ehlert thinks now, in autumn 1944 but refrains from exclaiming: 'I knew it!' He does not want to appear as a know-it-all in Burr's estimation once again.

The guard delivers his valuable cargo to a very small camp, where the two aviators meet other German prisoners for the first time. These men, tank crews, infantry soldiers, medics and pioneers, look dishevelled. All those among this bunch who are still able to walk more or less approach Ehlert and Burr. The aviators cannot believe it and look at each other in bafflement: the trench warriors beg for bread. They readily share with the infantrymen the bulk of their provisions, given to them at the command post. Burr and Ehlert have not known hunger so far. The whole scenario leaves a glum, depressing impression on the two aviators. During his encounter with these tattered comrades, Ehlert feels shame. He is ashamed to be a prisoner and foresees where his road will lead him. Until now being a prisoner has been a walk in the park, the Nagant on his chest aside. Here and now captivity becomes a stain, the mark of Cain.

The men spend the night in a barn bedded on hay. The infantrymen and tank crews sing weepy songs of home. The aviators feel a little bit left out. That is the worst: not to belong. This is something Burr and Ehlert will have to learn during the next weeks. The warm, sentimental and sad mood in this barn and the sense of loneliness will never leave the young Leutnant nor his gunner ever again. A sense of desperate helplessness comes over them, the feeling of being altogether forsaken, at the enemy's mercy without an idea of the future, with the thought of having to stay here forever, here in enemy country. Merely the memory of home, of the beloved Riele and the blonde Linda in Mergelstetten near Heidenheim, still waiting for Burr on the bank of the little romantic River Brenz, of their relatives and everything linked to them keeps the two aviators' hope alive.

The next morning the long journey farther east commences. The train stops at many small and large stations. Ehlert and Burr learn to be cold during the night and hungry during the day and to tremble and pray in secret during the remaining time. And they think of home, of how the current state has come about.

Through his father, Ehlert was connected to the military from early on. He thinks of the many posts he experienced during his young life due to his father's many transfers, for example the town of Rathenow at the River Havel, the global hub for the manufacture of spectacles. Large factories such as Nitsche and Günther are located there. Numerous small, even tiny family enterprises produce glasses. Emil Busch, an optical instruments factory, made binoculars, mainly 6 × 30. At Rathenow was the staff of the 3rd Cavalry Regiment with its commander Colonel Feldt. The trumpet corps was led by the bandmaster Sillig. Ehlert's father had meanwhile been promoted to staff sergeant and thus was counted among the senior non-commissioned officers. He carried a sabre with a golden pommel in the shape of a lion's head with red glass eyes.

In Rathenow, Gerhard attended the Reform Realgymnasium (secondary school). He had to catch up on two years of French. Latin was only taught in the higher classes. For his father this was the reason to pull him out of the junior organisation of the Hitler Youth without asking Gerhard first. Within three months Gerhard had made up the backlog. He received tuition from the student teacher Deneke, with whom learning was great fun. Deneke was inspiring. In his sparse lodgings the two loudly sang the Marseillaise, accompanied by Deneke at the piano. Thanks to his knowledge of Latin, Gerhard found it easy to learn French. Deneke always took a great interest in the grades of Gerhard's written work, and the latter never disappointed him. However, shortly after his teacher died of tuberculosis.

At that time Gerhard played second violin in the orchestra. His schoolmate Harry Keems, also in the orchestra, but playing lead violin, gave him a useful tip of how a vibrato had to be played, namely by adapting it to the mood of the musical piece. Gerhard took this hint seriously and cultivated the method during the course of his musical practice. Later fellow musicians told him independently from each other that he had a very beautiful tone. Ehlert knew to whom he owed this fact. From now on, he critically assessed all great violinists and even more all cellists in the manner in which they played a vibrato. Many did so as if there was only one way, very fast, regardless whether it was fitting or not.

Gerhard received violin lessons from Bandmaster Sillig. In retrospect Ehlert knows that he did not have a very good teacher in the latter. Sillig wholeheartedly represented the old school: a small cushion had to be tucked under the right upper arm at all times in order to loosen the wrist. He played études, yes, but he was not introduced to violin literature. What use was it therefore that Sillig, like all bandmasters, had studied at the renowned music academy of Berlin directed by the violin genius Joseph Joachim? Perhaps he could boast that he was a 'student grandson' of Joachim. His violin play would have improved vastly with a really capable teacher. His weekly lesson began with him having to fetch buns from a bakery. He practised half an hour a day, which was actually too little.

Gerhard did not stay at home during the summer holidays, but travelled to Meiersberg. First he took the train to Berlin. There he was welcomed by Aunt Bine, an older sister of his mother. They took the tram to Szczecin station and from there the journey continued by train for 151km to Ferdinandshof. He knew every stop. At the urban stations little carts with food and drink were pushed along the train, and delicacies such as '*Eberswalde cruller*' were called out. At Ferdinandshof, either a horse-drawn cart was waiting for him to take him to Meiersberg, or Walter Blankenburg came in his Chevrolet.

His relatives made no fuss about his visits. He joined the ranks of the gymnastics club every year. If the weather was fine they went to the beach, the seaside resort at the lagoon by Ueckermünde. To reach it, they cycled through the forest. Hundreds of bikes could be found on the parking lot, not one of them locked.

If required he washed at the pump while his cousin Inge cranked the handle. The cows were milked three times a day shortly after calving, then only in the morning and evening. In the morning Aunt Meta gave him a cup of milk still warm from the cow. His task was to fetch wood for the stove and to place it neatly inside its box next to the stove. At that time there still existed in some old farmhouses quaint stoves that were actually more like brick-built tables. The families cooked on an open fire with the pots and pans placed on cast-iron tripods. The smoke escaped though a funnel-shaped flue. Then brick-built stoves sprang up with closed fire pits covered by a cast-iron plate with circular openings. These contained several movable rings that could be removed depending on the size of the pot or pan.

After each milking Gerhard had to turn the centrifuge in which the milk was skimmed. This was in fact the first machine meant to ease the farmers' labour. Yet it did not bring much relief, as it had to be thoroughly cleaned after each use. This was laborious due to the many tapered plates. This task was the duty of Gerhard's ten-year-old cousin Inge.

His mother told him that in her youth – around 1900 – a so-called milk cabinet existed, made safe against cats by closely placed vertical rods, with many shelves on which were placed very shallow bowls filled with milk.

The cream settled at the top and could be scooped up and turned into butter. The skimmed milk was given to the cattle. In the butter tub, a tall tubular wooden vessel, butter was churned with a masher, a circular wooden disc with holes fixed to a handle. During thunderstorms no butter could be churned at all. Cold water was added and watered down the beautiful butter milk.

Meiersberg was also associated with the twittering of swallows, which had their nests in the stables and under roof overhangs, the sounds of the pigs, cows and the mother hen with her chicks, which were housed in a wire cage to protect them against cats and birds of prey. His mother also told him that in her youth a marksmen's festival was held every year. In the morning a brass band marched through the village as a wake-up call. In the afternoon everybody marched to the forest, at the front the brass band, then the girls in white dresses, after them the boys with their blow pipes to which they attached red roses. The girls threw a ball at a bird on a perch. Every hit dislodged a piece and the girl hitting the last piece became queen. His mother once succeeded herself. The boys aimed at a disc with their blow pipes and the best became king of marksmen.

Gerhard celebrated marksmen's festivals in Meiersberg, too. He asked for some money from his relatives. There was a carousel powered by two boys. In the centre, hidden by wooden planks, was a cross of wooden beams that had to be pushed by two strong lads. For this deed they received a free ride.

There was also a post mill in Meiersberg. Gerhard never forgot the scent and the floorboards smoothed by flour and grain, the creaking of the wooden cog wheels. The miller, Hermann Krüger, was also a baker. You could purchase bread without cash. A sack of grain was driven to the mill in a wheelbarrow, and in return one received sixty loaves of bread. If a loaf of bread was fetched, the miller kept the tally in a blue notebook. After sixty tallies another sack of grain was brought to the mill.

Sometimes Gerhard also slept at his Aunt Erna's house, his mother's oldest sister, in the gable room of the attic. This room was in the east and he was woken by the sun. If there was an easterly wind and very warm temperatures the scent of resin from the forest flooded the room.

In spring 1936 he rejoined the junior organisation of the Hitler Youth, after he had not been 'organised' for two years and two months. Service in this NSDAP youth organisation was boring. He took part in two camps, and one of them he recalled vividly. It started one Friday with fine weather.

Gerhard and nine other boys, almost all in the same class, decided during break to journey to Pritzerbe the next day. This location is situated at a Havel lake south-east of Rathenow. They decided who would bring what, assisted by the good advice of their mothers: one took care of the ingredients for their meals, one of the large aluminium pot, another of the then popular type of jam. Members of the junior organisation could borrow tent squares.

So they set off, not because they were ordered to, but out of mere fancy. Having reached their destination, two boys cycled into the village to ask a farmer for straw as padding for their tent – everything proper and civilised. The tent squares were buttoned together. After the tent had been erected, a ditch had to be dug all around it to protect against potential rain (they knew it would not rain, but rules are rules). The job done, they ate jam sandwiches and drank barley coffee.

What else needed to be done? They tried to scout out if there were other groups camping nearby whom one could visit during the night. Then they intended to pull out all the tent pegs simultaneously so that the tent would collapse. That was a harmless prank, but great fun for those awaiting the effect of their deed from a safe distance. Unfortunately they did not find other groups.

In the afternoon they dug a circular trench and lit a small fire in its centre that was not supposed to go out during the night. Two boys each took turn to collect dry wood in the forest. It got dark. Night watches were assigned. Everyone had to stand guard for one hour, armed with a spear. The worst was the watch between 2am and 3am. One had to go into the forest in deep darkness to fetch more wood for the fire. Suddenly one heard a crunching noise. Horror of horrors! A person, an enemy? Hopefully just an animal.

In the morning they performed gymnastics, then they ran naked through the forest to the lake for a swim. The next afternoon they had to dismantle everything and return the straw. Such carefree days were retained in the memory like a wonderful vacation today. It was simply romantic. Experiences like this contributed to having romanticised memories of one's time of youth.

Much that happened at that time was received quite positively by most people. For example, Hitler managed to overcome the immense unemployment in a relatively short period. Most did not notice that this was done by means of a gigantic armaments programme. It rather stirred up satisfaction that this was against the hated Versailles Treaty. Hitler, however, already thought further than the mass of the population during those years. His programme not only intended the revision of the peace treaty of Versailles, so adverse to Germany, but also the conquest of new 'living space' in the east – of course at the cost of the people living there, who were decried as inferior.

The millions of unemployed did not care whether they worked at an arms factory or built strategically important transport routes somewhere else, the main thing was that they had work again with which they could sustain their families.

In addition, Hitler made Germans felt empowered again. The working class in particular felt more valued, since the NSDAP called all employed persons 'workers' and only differentiated between the 'worker of the brow' and the 'worker of the fist' in the pathos common for that time. This was received none too badly within the working class who traditionally leaned towards the Social Democrats and Communists. In his speeches, Hitler drilled into the Germans as a whole that they were the most industrious and in every respect best people on earth, which flattered the more simple-minded in particular. In Meiersberg, Gerhard himself experienced that from about 1936 onward the critical attitude towards National Socialism by his diehard Social Democrat relatives was gradually replaced with a more positive assessment. After all: 'He really does something for the working class', was the refrain. Only Ehlert's mother was not impressed and persevered unwaveringly in her rejection, whether out of spite or out of instinct. Gerhard was thus influenced from many sides, so that in spite of his parents' influence he no longer viewed Hitler and his regime so negatively.

On 28 February 1937 Gerhard was confirmed at his church. Dean Heimerdinger taught the confirmation classes. He always began his lessons by taking off his jacket, putting down his pocket watch and performing a handstand. He was known for climbing onto the high dive board at the swimming pool, performing a handstand at the top and walking on his hands to the edge of the board before jumping.

At confirmation presents are received and Gerhard received a wrist watch, a pocket book with his initials from Uncle Alfred and Aunt Elsbet Scherping from Spandau – he was staff manager for German Lufthansa – and several gifts of money, in total 85 Marks. With this he bought a Panther brand bicycle manufactured in Rathenow. It was later stolen in Brunswick. That was not a great nuisance since its tyres had 26½in tyres and one could no longer buy tubes soon after, as they were replaced by those of 26 or 28in.

Ehlert has a lot of time right now to think and his memories of his childhood and youth keep him warm inside. They are taken farther and farther into the east. The train stops at numerous stations, large and small. At the end of their journey begins a new one, much longer and more brutal: captivity in the Red Army camps. Yet at first fate means well for the two of them.

5

Land of Milk and Honey

The carriages roll ponderously over the Russian tracks. The smoke of the locomotive flies past them. Kilometre by kilometre they travel farther into the lair of Josef Stalin, deeper and deeper. Once a day the German prisoners receive the bare necessities. There is still bread and water, the train still stops every now and again, and the few guard details open the doors and let in fresh, cool autumn air. The captives relieve themselves en route through a hole in the bottom of the carriage.

They make only slow progress. Time and again their train has to be diverted when a troop transport or a freight train for the front comes their way. The fighting Red Army takes priority over the Wehrmacht soldiers rolling towards captivity. Therefore it takes days until they reach their first destination, Camp 27, Krasnogorsk west of Moscow. Somehow the German prisoners – in the meantime Ehlert and Burr have become part of a larger group of thirty or forty men – do not seem to have been expected here. The camp commander has no use for the new arrivals as his camp has been overcrowded since Stalingrad. To begin with, the German aviators are quarantined and for the first time they make the acquaintance of the Russians' re-education measures. For now these are still pitiful, sometimes downright comical, attempts. Here at Krasnogorsk, Ehlert and Burr hear the first of those long-winded speeches that will be repeated in all Russian prison camps. It is given by a German officer in a black tank uniform, General Martin Lattmann. Some of his men do not believe their eyes and ears. The formerly diehard Nazi and party member, who on 2 February 1943 on his own authority as major general ordered the surrender of the northern cauldron of Stalingrad to the Red Army, was one of the first here at Krasnogorsk to defect to the Communists. Now he preaches to the men of Germany's depravity and Hitler's dictatorship.

'General Sir, this sounded quite differently at the artillery school Jüterbog where as a lieutenant colonel you were my instructor,' mocks one of his tank crews, for which he receives jeering applause. Lattmann is so ashamed by the encounter with one of his recruits here that he goes red in the face and begins to stammer. Ehlert does not care. He no longer listens and experiences the following days in the totally overcrowded camp as in a trance. He and Burr lose sight of each other time and again, but manage to find each other somehow. They have grown into companions of fate in some kind of manner. And yet the two continue to be on formal terms, almost a little distant. The young Leutnant will never offer the informal address to his Unteroffizier. Ehlert did not like bonhomie as a civilian and likes it even less as a soldier.

In the barracks where Ehlert sits tight on his berth, he is a popular go-to guy. Most soldiers relate pilots with planes, and planes with the best chance of running away. And so a German staff surgeon and a radio communicator use all their powers of persuasion on the young aviator to join an escape with them to an airfield near Moscow. All three of them start to hoard bread. After all, they do not wish to starve during their escape.

Yet Ehlert gets cold feet after a few days. Again, his common sense prevails and he eventually convinces the hotheads of the futility of their plan. 'Supposing we manage to escape, we creep up to the airfield and chose a twin-engine aircraft that has just been refuelled. We somehow manage to get inside the plane, too. And then? Then I have to know where the main lever is for starting the entire electrics. Even if I find it, who will start the engine for us? With the Luftwaffe, you need a battery wagon for this to provide the power for ignition. This won't be much different with a Russian aircraft. To be honest, this plan has no chance.'

Ehlert shakes his head, and the other two daredevils hang theirs. Another escape plan here in Krasnogorsk will not come about. The next morning Ehlert's and Burr's group is transferred. They are driven by truck to Kazan on the River Volga, 500km east of Moscow. The mighty river, the stream of fate that broke the German 6th Army in the winter of 1942–43 at Stalingrad, comes into view from the elevated east bank. Its waters resemble an immense lake. Upriver, at this spot, the Volga is much wider than it is 1,000km south at Stalingrad. The mighty stream burns breathtaking images into the men's minds. And then the two German aviators and their fellow prisoners almost have to laugh when the three trucks stop at the harbour. In front of them lies an old steamboat that will be their next transport. 'It is almost like a holiday trip', Burr jokes, and Ehlert lets slip a broad grin.

From Kazan they travel downriver to the mouth of the tributary Kama, and the old boat steams up this river to a place that will be their prison for a long time: Yelabuga.

The small episcopal town lies 960km east of Moscow. In autumn 1944 red banners adorn the squat white houses. The former monastery, built in the eighteenth century by Italian architects, serves as a prison camp. Since the revolution, however, the buildings have lacked all adornment, that was completely removed by the Communists. Between the two churches on the river's high bank, the central administrative bodies of the NKVD are found. This is the abbreviation for *Narodnyj komissariat wnutriennich del*, the Russian Ministry of the Interior, with its entire secret police apparatus that is feared throughout Russia in all places and at all times, not only by the German captives. Of course, this apparatus also exists in Yelabuga.

The steamboat with the German prisoners berths at a rusty quay. Grumpily and almost a little impatiently, Ehlert and Burr together with the others trudge up the hill into the town and finally into the monastery. In a courtyard, where the small German group – the two aviators among them – comes to its first halt during this sunny morning, bullet holes in the walls commemorate the murder of Czarist cadets.

While looking through the open windows, Ehlert notices naked, emaciated men. They throw long shadows during their morning ablutions. Many of them are at some task, on the march to somewhere or making their beds. There is a busy atmosphere, but not hectic. This calms Ehlert for now. Together with the other new arrivals, he has to undergo the usual 'auspice'. They have to take off jackets, waistcoats, shirts and shifts and stretch out their arms away from their bodies. 'Lift your wings,' one of the prisoners complains, standing with Ehlert and Burr in the monastery's courtyard, amused and irritated at the same time. The Russians look for tattooed numbers at the bottom of the upper arms near the armpits. All members of the Waffen-SS received a tattoo with their blood type there. The hated SS soldiers are picked out from the remaining troops.

The small group of prisoners has already had to endure this examination several times during the previous days, so all are confident that none of them will fall through the cracks. Then they continue into another courtyard. There the prisoners' hair is shaved off. For the scalp this is done by a hairdresser. Yet it causes some muttering that the men have to undress completely – and that in front of Russian women's eyes. The latter are standing ready with scissors and remove the Germans' pubic hair.

And then the daily routine in the Yelabuga camp begins, which Ehlert and Burr need some time to get used to. They realise how lucky they have been so far. Among the first fellow prisoners whose acquaintance they make is a paymaster. He is one of the 'Stalingrad men'. For a long time, this is something special among all the German prisoners. A touch of heroism and sacrifice surrounds the Stalingrad men. The paymaster tells the two aviators of the downfall of the 6th Army in the city at the Volga. The infantry officers had stayed inside their safe bunkers during the battle for the city, and the quartermasters and paymasters had to bring provisions to them by fighting through the storm of steel of the Russian artillery.

Ehlert and Burr listen in awe, but say nothing. Only a few days later they know that their silence was a good thing. They learn from other Stalingrad men that hardly any infantry officer has survived the battle of encirclement – but a disproportionate number of paymasters, surgeons and clergymen.

The two newcomers are already more cautious when they hear the next stories, and yet everyone listens mesmerised when Stalingrad men talk of their capture: how after their capitulation the Russians drove them from the basements into the icy cold of February, how they had to march in long columns, how the first men, being too feeble, were left behind at the sides of their road.

'At the beginning the Russians were still merciful and put an end to the men's suffering by a shot in the neck. When the numbers became higher, they let those remaining behind at the roadside simply freeze to death', an officer from Stalingrad relates. You can still tell the hardships of these first weeks of his captivity and the marching through the winter to the camps in the east from looking at him, even one and a half years after his capture. He looks the age of a lieutenant colonel. Although he is perhaps in his early thirties, his hair is grey, his face pallid and around his eyes is a despair that no longer allows him to smile. It will never let him smile again.

'For weeks they chased us through the snow without equipment, without provisions and without sanitation. We will never forget that miserable cold. At night we banded together in circles. Those at the centre managed to get through the night alright. Those outside had frozen to death by morning. We left them behind like a silent memorial when we were driven farther.'

In silence and shock the aviators digest the tales and can hardly believe how simple and without problems was their capture in contrast. For this thought Ehlert immediately apologises to his dead and – to his knowledge – missing crew members.

Ehlert and Burr part company over the next few days. The pilot loses sight of his gunner more and more. In Yelabuga a strict separation of squad, non-commissioned officers and commissioned officers prevails. The latter are the majority among the captives. The old monastery gradually turns exclusively into an officers' camp. Ehlert accepts the separation from his comrade with some melancholy. How often fate could have separated them already, how often a Russian bullet, how often a mere coincidence. They have overcome everything together so far, and now they are torn apart just because their ranks are different. At least he is still alive, Ehlert thinks. Perhaps he is an alright chap after all, the old know-it-all, Burr grins to himself and then sighs so quietly that nobody can hear him.

While the two German aviators settle into their daily life at the prison camp as best as they can, thousands of soldiers are dying daily at the Eastern Front. It is autumn 1944. The large-scale Russian offensive, the preparation for which the long-range reconnaissance aviators could construe from the thousands of artillery pieces and tanks prior to their crash, is in full swing. The German southern front has collapsed, and the Red Army is heading for Hungary and Romania.

In the meantime, the Russians have gained much experience in the administration of their victory. They are expecting many new prisoners, including at Yelabuga, and therefore room is made within the monastery complex. And so at the beginning of October, Ehlert is transferred to the main camp, the so-called Kama camp: another monastery with three churches. The German pilot is at first assigned to a berth in the auditorium, in which several dozens of captives are accommodated. Opposite him lies Ernst Mietzner, a guard officer from Gegensee. This is a village 18km east of Meiersberg. It is a small world, even in the middle of Russia. The two make friends with each other and Mietzner makes a metal spoon for Ehlert, who only owns a primitive wooden one. Ordnance officers have a knack for metal and other intricate work.

Ehlert finds more comrades with whom he feels connected during the first days. He learns that his schoolmate Wolfgang Scheller is in Yelabuga, too. And he hears of the son of his teacher, Dr Wüster. It is the latter he subsequently encounters and the two men develop an intimate friendship from the start. Unfortunately, Wüster has sad news to impart to Ehlert first. Wolfgang Scheller, who was in the same unit as Wüster, fell at Stalingrad, bleeding to death from a wound from a tiny bullet that had scratched the artery of the lower abdomen.

Ehlert's mood swings wildly from depression to euphoria during the following days. How long will he and his comrades be held captive here? Until the end of the war? Until eternity? Again he feels quite helpless, being at his enemies' mercy, without knowing what the future will bring. Again he misses his home and most of all his Riele, who still does not know what has happened to him. Ehlert and his crew have been reported missing, that much has already been communicated at home. The uncertainty is torture for the young woman at home, although if she knew where he was she may have been relieved. For her beloved is at that moment most certainly better protected in the Yelabuga monastery than in any section of the Eastern Front, or inside any plane over Russia. She just does not know it.

On the other hand, Ehlert suspects he is lucky. During the following days he looks for familiar faces and after a short while several groups take care of him. For example, there are eight prisoners from Göttingen in Yelabuga. Göttingen is one of the many posts of Ehlert's military family. Gerhard's father was transferred there in 1937, as the 3rd Cavalry Regiment, though connected to the Mark Brandenburg for several centuries, was to be deployed to Göttingen.

During the first days in Yelabuga the young pilot has much time at his hands to recall the two years in Göttingen and to exchange news with his fellow prisoners from there. He still remembers vividly the considerable adjustment the move to Göttingen meant for the entire family. His father's term of service ended after twelve years on 30 September 1937, just ten days after their move to Göttingen. A new position had to be found.

At that time four mess halls were built for the new barracks, two each for one brigade. Innumerable applications were made for the two canteen manager positions, and the commander could make the decision without any restrictions. He decided in favour of his chauffeur of many years, a man named Rosenmüller, and of Ehlert's father, the former corps leader of the trumpet corps.

Ehlert's mother was as keen as mustard and implored her husband to accept the offer and not to withdraw under any circumstance, just because he might not feel up to the challenge. She viewed this as their great chance to earn lots of money. Therefore his father decided to accept the position. His mother promptly contributed ideas and plans for the future, but was not able to overcome the bureaucratic hurdles. However, after the enterprise had been running for a year, it was evident that Ehlert's mess hall ran smoothly, while Rosenmüller's enterprise experienced difficulties. As a result, his rival threw in the towel soon after.

Once again it became evident that Ehlert's father had the talent to come to grips with a new challenge quickly and successfully. After their meal, the soldiers bum-rushed the canteen counter directly next to the dining hall and ordered beer and cake. The product range on offer included cigarettes, pencils, stationary, shoe brushes, fountain pens, sabres, aprons, gun oil and hundreds of other items.

Ehlert has to smile to himself, as he is lying on his berth in the auditorium, staring at the ceiling and thinking of his father's canteen. Cake and coffee could be ordered, fried potatoes and eggs. At convivial gatherings, so-called boot drinking games were played where the boot was a two-litre glass in the shape of this item of apparel.

The curfew was strictly obeyed at the Göttingen barracks and the sergeant of the guard – an figure of absolute authority – made sure of this. Everything was orderly routine. The canteen manager's family actually had their own telephone. Now, seven years after his stay at Göttingen, Ehlert could still remember the number: 2647. After curfew, calls were redirected from the mess hall to their private apartment.

In the light of their prosperous situation, the family bought a large radio. One evening Gerhard, who had just turned fifteen years old, heard the overture from Richard Wagner's opera *Tannhäuser*. He was deeply impressed and so his entry into a new world of music began. In the evenings he carried the radio to his night stand and looked through the radio programme for broadcasts with Wagner music. In addition, he bought booklets from the Reclam press with the lyrics of all the musical dramas. Soon after he discovered Tchaikovsky and was fascinated. As a result he began to listen in earnest to the music of the Romantic period.

In contrast, his mother spent much of her day reading in her armchair. She only worked part-time at the mess hall since most of the tasks were performed by their employees. Four of them came from Meiersberg. The slightly isolated location of their apartment allowed Ehlert's mother to listen regularly to London's 'enemy broadcast' on the BBC, which became a punishable offence at the outbreak of war. Without having to fear informers as neighbours, night after night Ehlert's mother listened to the British news.

Furthermore, she made a habit of talking frequently to the soldiers coming from the front. She questioned them in an innocuous manner, but quite deliberately, and filtered out the real situation. Within their family Ehlert's mother always called Hitler 'the devil in disguise', and she adhered to her opinion even when the 'greatest field commander of all times' was at the height of his popularity after the Wehrmacht's victory over France. In Ehlert's father's view Hitler was just the 'Bohemian private' about whom he only spoke in derogatory terms.

Ehlert's room was the only one facing the forest, where 200m away there was a popular pub, the Kaiser-Wilhelm-Park. Light music for dancing reached his ears, and in a melancholic mood he now recalls this lying on his berth. When he continues to think of Göttingen, the hills and little mountains spring foremost to his mind. The highest peak in the vicinity was the Hoher Hagen at 508m and in the south, 33km away, the Hoher Meißner at 754m. He did not like this hilly landscape very much as the peaks obstructed his view, he being a son of the flat Meiersberg on the Baltic Sea. And the town itself, with its narrow streets, a tiny market square, and worst of all ugly churches, did not leave a favourable impression on the young Gerhard. He was used to the large brick churches of northern Germany with their tall, slim towers and the colourful narrow windows. Yet how he longed to see Göttingen's ugly churches now instead of having to stare at the ceiling in this remote monastery in the middle of Russia.

At that time Gerhard was already used to changing schools frequently. Every time a new teacher entered the classroom he put his hand up, stood up and repeated the standard phrase: 'I have recently joined this class.' Ehlert attended was called Kaiser-Wilhelm-II Secondary School in Göttingen and but soon after it was renamed 'Secondary School for Boys', since the monarchy and the emperor Wilhelm II in particular were not highly regarded in the Nazi empire.

The school's requirements were tough, and new students usually received the worst grades in all subjects. A high standard of teaching quality was easily achieved, since Göttingen University provided a plethora of junior teachers as many graduates liked the town and wished to stay. The board of education thus had a wide choice for new recruits among the best candidates.

Before the Second World War one could obtain a licence for motorcycles when aged sixteen. Therefore, a few days after his birthday, Ehlert went to a policeman he knew and promptly received his after he had answered a few questions correctly. Although Ehlert's father was very careful with his money, he bought his son a NSU-Quick motorcycle with a 98cc engine, a rather slow model, for 290 Marks. In the summer of 1939 he took a ride on this bike to Cologne, along the Rhine and the Moselle, to Frankfurt, Heidelberg, Bamberg, Coburg, Würzburg and the Thuringian Forest. Gerhard did not know that this would be his last journey in peacetime. On 1 September 1939 war broke out, and no fuel was available for private motorcycles.

Ehlert's parents owned an Opel Super 6 with a 2.5l engine of 55hp at that time. This stately car managed a top speed of 130km/h. The family owned the car for roughly a year before they had to cede it to the Wehrmacht, and it remained at the Göttingen barracks. A few days later soldiers entered the mess hall and, grinning widely, asked Ehlert's father: 'Would you like to see your car now?' There stood the formerly gleaming white car and it was hardly recognisable for it had received camouflage painting.

At that time Ehlert began to take an interest in the Hitler Youth and there was a lot on offer in the organisation. One could choose according to one's interests: motorcycling, flying a glider, rowing, model construction, radio communication, drama groups, fanfare corps, marching band, string orchestra etc. Ehlert dedicated his time until his military service to music. Every Tuesday evening they met in the school auditorium to play music in the Hitler Youth district orchestra. Here the older cohorts from the school orchestras of the three grammar schools came together: Ehlert's school, the Classical Languages Grammar School and the Lyceum. The conductor was the music teacher, a very tall man who was as thin as a rail called Rehkopf (deer head) who customarily wore a Hitler Youth uniform.

Ehlert almost has to laugh thinking about his music teacher with the peculiar name. And since he is in the process of contemplating his youth, he now tells his bunk neighbour in the Yelabuga monastery of his athletic achievements. At the regional athletic competitions held in Hanover, twice – in 1939 and 1940 – he became regional champion of Lower Saxony in paramilitary sports. This was a form of paramilitary training invented by the Nazis for their future soldiers. It comprised four disciplines: 25km of forced march, then 15km target shooting with a small-calibre rifle at a distance of 25m followed immediately by a 200m obstacle course. 'Murderous' slips out of Ehlert's mouth. Long throwing with clubs came at the conclusion of the competition. Of course – Ehlert realised this from the first day – all this was for military purposes. Later during the war this paramilitary training became mandatory for young people – for many perhaps a reason to take up a military career later on.

And now? Now the war is lost, as certain as night follows day. He – Ehlert – would no longer have a part in it at any rate, of this the young man on his bunk is certain. And although he has just stared at the ceiling with a smile on his lips and exchanged merry memories with his bunk neighbour, he promptly falls into a dark hole again. Where will it all end? What will become of him? Damned war!

And again he thinks of home. The eight prisoners from Göttingen in Yelabuga have a share in this just like a few aviators with whom he went to war college and who are now prisoners just like him. And there is a third group in Yelabuga to which he feels attached: the cavalrymen from the 3rd Regiment, to which his father had belonged before the war, and which had become part of the 24th Tank Division. Due to tradition the men wore their black tank uniform with gold piping, signifying the good old cavalry.

With the aid of men from all three groups looking after the young pilot, Ehlert is initiated into the important matters of camp life during these first days. There is, for example, the 'National Committee for a Free Germany', an organisation brought into being by the Russians in 1943 after their victory at Stalingrad. The Soviets gave the emigrant Walter Ulbricht the task of enlisting support for it within the prisoner of war camps. For captured officers a subsidiary organisation was founded called 'League of German Officers' (LGO). The two organisations had in common that their members had denounced Nazi Germany and in return they received many privileges. In the eyes of the other captives in Yelabuga, just like in all other camps, they were nothing but rotten traitors who became turncoats now that they were at the Russians' mercy. 'Opportunists!' rant those who refuse to join the National Committee.

Outwardly the two hostile groups within the camp are easily distinguished; Those who do not join keep their insignia of eagle and swastika. Members wear three stripes in the colours of the former empire – black, white, and red – instead of the Nazi insignia. This was introduced by the Russians as well as the weekly newspaper *Free Germany*, which is available to members of the National Committee and framed in these colours.

The very first day Ehlert realises how hostile both groups are to each other. They do not wish each other a happy birthday or even light each other's cigarettes. In order to receive one of the desirable postings in the kitchen, the bakery or the laundry one has to be a member of the National Committee or the LGO. Ehlert longs to play in the camp orchestra, but for this he would have to denounce his comrades and this is out of the question for the Luftwaffe Leutnant – at least for now.

During that time a delegation of the International Red Cross is expected at Yelabuga for an inspection of the officers' camp. On this occasion Ehlert learns for the first time the difference between the Russian and the German mentality. The German officers have their meals in a beautiful vaulted cellar, with its end wall decorated with scenes from German fairy tales. As the Russian camp commanders are afraid that the Red Cross might object to the quality of the bowls, the camp metalworking shop is supposed to manufacture new metal ones. But where to find the metal? There the Russians show themselves to be resourceful. As it has not rained during the last few days, the monastery roof's zinc plate is unceremoniously removed. Now the German prisoners are able to eat their thin soup from brand new zinc bowls, which is not particularly helpful, since food remains a problem for a long time. Most of the time there is only bread and water.

Weeks pass, and the first Russian winter in captivity at Yelabuga looms over the German officers. For now none of them suspects how lucky they are to be spending their time there. Many of them, among them Gerhard Ehlert, will have to pay for going to war for Hitler's Nazi Germany in totally different conditions.

It is the beginning of December 1944 when Ehlert feels for the first time what it means to be at someone's mercy. According to international law, captive officers must not be forced into labour and so far the Russians have conformed to this. There is no boredom though. Those who do not belong to the LGO are excluded from many offerings within the camp, because only members of the National Committee are allowed to learn Russian, for example. All the same, there is a kind of lecture programme for all prisoners in Latin, English, French, maths and history, and there is a German library. Never again in his life will Ehlert master the three languages he had learned at school so well as here in Yelabuga. For the entire autumn he almost feels comfortable within these venerable abbey walls. He could almost forget the surrounding barbed wire if there was not the constant longing for home.

During this time Gerhard is exceedingly busy. He composes a short piece of music and learns the entire prose poem 'Cornet' by Rilke. Rilke's text becomes a myth for the young officer. In this he is joined by many of his contemporaries. The copy Ehlert finds in the library contains a dried rose petal and the words of a lover to her beloved called to the front. What is described in the 'Cornet' can be felt outside the book, too. The identification is perfect. Inspired by Rilke, the young pilot composes two volumes of poems and becomes intimately acquainted with musical theory. Then Advent 1944 approaches and Mozart's Serenade No. 13 is performed publicly. There are so many musicians in the camp that Mozart's composition is played by three sets of them.

Of equal strength is the well-organised network of informers. In every dorm room there is at least one person who reports regularly to the German camp command about each and everything within his dorm. This news is then forwarded to the Russian political officer. However, most of the time it does not take long for the informer to be unmasked. When he is on his way to the German camp command, the others shout after him: 'Well, we hope you haven't forgotten anything important!'

Small amounts of bread are stolen quite frequently but the guilty are found quickly. In most cases they are those who fetch bread from the cutting room, where the bread is divided into 300g portions. If the cutting leads to a smaller amount, small scraps are fixed to the larger piece of bread with a kind of toothpick. These additional pieces are often devoured during transport. Those caught in this act naturally receive punishment. You can always find someone who will smack the guilty party on the naked bottom. Repeat offenders, however, are not let off with a few red weals. The thief is dragged to the hairdresser, who shaves off his hair. All the camp inmates see the shaven head, so the thief cannot hide and is stigmatised for the near future.

All the prisoners still wear their German uniforms with rank insignia and awards at that time. In Yelabuga many Knight's Crosses are dangling around throats. Yet that will change quickly. Until then, however, Ehlert and his fellow prisoners still have a slack, almost tranquil period. Even during Christmas 1944, when it could be supposed that the prisoners suffer all the more from homesickness, turns into a celebration that nobody present will ever forget. The large auditorium, which is entered through three tall doors, is decorated with fir green. After dinner the prisoners celebrate a church service in the auditorium. Then the officers retreat to their dorms. A Christmas tree is found in each of them. For months two doctors gathered empty vials, which now serve as candles. They are filled with petroleum and sport a tiny wick. Christmas songs are sung. Santa Claus roams about with his bag of presents. Everyone has prepared a gift for another, which Santa then distributes. Ehlert receives a self-made sewing and darning needle from an anonymous donor. It must have taken weeks to fashion the eye by constant rubbing of the wire. Shortly before midnight the camp choir of eighty men sings Christmas songs ringing through the vast building. On Christmas Day the men are woken by the camp brass orchestra playing 'Vom Himmel hoch' (From Heaven Above). Tears flow.

Yet there are less pleasant moments. At the beginning of January 1945, Ehlert's dorm of forty men is quarantined as there is a suspicion that there has been an outbreak of diphtheria. All these men are accommodated in a small house near the monastery. One of them is smart enough to quickly grab Homer's *Odyssey* from the library. After all, the prisoners are not allowed to leave the house for four weeks while under quarantine. The very first day of their isolation they organise a skat (popular German card game) tournament. Doppelkopf (another popular card game), bridge and chess are also played. When the men are lying on their bunks in the evening, an oil lamp is lit and one of the prisoners reads aloud from the *Odyssey* – just so much that they reach the last page at the end of their forty days. Ehlert is haunted by the description of sunrise: 'And when Eos, the goddess of dawn, woke with her rose fingers ...' It is as if they were on the beach of an Aegean island. And even after their quarantine the men remain close and continue their readings.

One evening, however, dark clouds gather over Yelabuga, which until now has been a land of milk and honey for Ehlert's mind, though not his stomach. A Russian non-commissioned officer enters their dorm and hammers home to Ehlert that he has to report for fetching wood from the forest the next morning. Of course, he does not go to the agreed meeting point out of spite. Yet he must pay for this instantly. Half an hour later the Russian soldier arrives to fetch him. Ehlert is thrown into the detention cell, a dark hole without a stove and without glass in its little window. At night the temperatures drop to -20 degrees, and Ehlert is left freezing miserably. Still borne by youthful naivety, he demands to speak to the Russian commander and promptly goes into hunger strike. Yet nothing happens. After three days and three icy nights, he emerges from the hole starving. He swings wildly between a triumphal and a wretched mood caused by cold and hunger. He has to end his hunger strike before getting too weak. In those days privates received ¾ litre of soup for breakfast and lunch, 150g gruel for lunch and

300 to 400g gruel for dinner. The gruel has the same taste as the soup, it is just slightly thicker. To cover themselves the men receive a coat.

Officers receive ¾ litre of soup for breakfast and lunch, plus 150g gruel for lunch and 300g gruel for dinner. In addition they also get 300g rye bread, 300g light bread and 30g butter and sugar each, the latter two items on the spot. The officers further receive fifteen cigarettes. A blanket and a coat serve as cover. To this is added a bed sheet and pillowcase for each man.

For a while it seems as if the German officer has had his way with his determination not to work. It is already April when he is summoned once more. The camp's inner zone is to be raked. This comprises the area between the two fences surrounding the camp, a distance of about 3 metres. Now that most of the snow has melted, it has to be raked thoroughly again. In that way the Russian guard posts can discern easily whether anybody has moved through it. Anybody climbing over the first fence leaves footprints inside the inner zone. Again Ehlert shows himself to be recalcitrant and refuses to pick up the rake. As long as he only receives bread and water, he is not able to work, he tells his Russian guards.

The unruly officer promptly ends up with the German camp commander, a major called Gottfried Mangold, bearer of the Knight's Cross, from Bodenwerder at the River Weser. The well-nourished man faces the young pilot, who at that point weighs less than 50 kilos.

'My dear man, why do you insist on not working?' the commander asks him.

'You know Stalin's Order No. 55 that German officers need not work,' replies Ehlert.

At this response the camp commander rolls his eyes: 'And what's the deal with your remark that you aren't able to work because of receiving only bread and water? Every day you receive soup and gruel.'

'Major Sir, I know this is rather pedantic, but for two months we have received neither butter nor sugar, and the soup and gruel contain rye flour. That is the same as the bread.'

The camp commander soon becomes aware that he cannot argue against that and that he will end up banging his head against a brick wall with Ehlert. However, the latter has to be made to realise in turn that the major has the upper hand. A few minutes after the unpleasant conversation the young pilot ends up in the detention cell again and stays there for several days.

6

Lost Years, Lost Compass

On 8 May 1945 an odd mood prevails within the camp. All are nervous, and rumours make the rounds. The evening news spoke of intense fighting in Berlin. At the end of the programme, a reference is made to a special broadcast scheduled for some time during the night. Nobody is able to sleep. Well after 10pm the Russian national anthem blares from the loudspeakers. The newsreader announces that Germany has surrendered, the Russian troops have gained a great victory, the arms have fallen silent and the war is over.

With tears in their eyes, silent in their shock and homesickness, but in the budding hope for an imminent end to their captivity, the men remain standing in the huge stairwell for a long time. Downcast, humiliated and shattered, they crawl to their bunks. Everybody is concerned with his own thoughts in this hour. What will the future bring? When will they go home? Questions upon questions, but no answers.

Ehlert is lying on his bunk and thinks of the past. Why oh why did he get so involved in this war that is now definitely lost? How had this come about? Only vaguely does he recall his childhood. The many professional transfers of his father come to mind. The frequent changes of scenery, which let them stay only briefly at any given place, entailed many changes of schools. He was hence not able to develop a sense of home as a child. At the beginning they moved into the first best apartment available, then into the next, and finally into a permanent one.

How quickly such transfers could come about is illustrated by the following affair: a war comrade of Gerhard's father, Erich Priem from Eichhof near Ferdinandshof, had the good fortune to serve with the Reichswehr in Rendsburg. He wrote to Gerhard's father that a position in the musical corps was available. His father travelled to Rendsburg, had an interview and was accepted. Twenty other applicants left empty-handed. These positions were very desirable, as one became a civil servant for twelve years and thus as good as impossible to dismiss.

The barracks were located at the River Eider, which was subject to the tides with a tidal range of 60cm. The river was less than 100m from Ehlerts' apartment and during low tide Gerhard could venture far. The non-commissioned officers and their families were living in a residential complex and there were many children around to play with. Most importantly, there were horses stabled, and where there are horses, there are also a smithy, a saddlery and cartwrights.

Rendsburg possessed only a small-scale barracks, where one squadron under the command of the cavalry captain Vogel was stationed. The latter's son Harro soon became friends with Gerhard. At his home they played with tin soldiers, and Harro's friendly mother provided the boys with hot chocolate. Captain Vogel was an enthusiastic hobby photographer. He owned a 9×12cm plate camera and had his own dark room. He took pictures of the children's birthday celebrations, for example. On one occasion Gerhard and his brother had to go outside with their sleigh during the winter of 1928–29 because a photograph showing the abundance of snow was to be taken.

Gerhard developed a particular passion for kites and toy bows. Arrows were fashioned from reeds growing along the Eider, their tips from elder wood.

A sensation in the children's eyes was their cart drawn by a billy goat. All barracks with horse stables had such a goat; perhaps it was there to ward off diseases with its pungent odour. The cartwrights built the cart and the saddlers fashioned the harness. When the boys wanted to drive the goat, they went to the stables. The young soldiers caught the goat, hitched it up and off they went. The boys had the entire barracks to themselves.

At that time a very special picture with the billy goat was taken: at the front of the cart sits Harro, at the back Gerhard and in the middle stands Dieter Zemke, the vet's son. In some sense it was a historic photograph, as all three of them became officers. In November 1943 Ehlert read in a newspaper that Harro Vogel, a Leutnant in the mechanised infantry, had fallen in Italy. Gerhard later made his first sortie with Dieter Zemke, who also became a pilot with the night time long-range reconnaissance troops and by pure chance the two childhood friends were deployed together.

A long railway bridge spanned the Kiel Canal near Rendsburg. With a clearance of 42m, it was to allow the passage of large warships. Thanks to this forward planning, large merchant ships are still able to use the world's busiest waterway today without difficulty. There was also a swivel bridge, which was later demolished. The liner SMS *Schleswig-Holstein* once berthed in

Rendsburg, too, which will play a special part later. Built in 1907, it took part in the First World War and fired the first shots of the Second when it enfiladed the Westerplatte at Gdansk. The Soviets later seized it as a war trophy.

Christmas 1926 left a very special impression on Gerhard, who was just four years old. All the families and their children gathered in a large room. Then Santa Claus came, a particularly tall soldier, wearing a long fur coat. He arrived in a horse-drawn sleigh and climbed through the tall window. For a long time Gerhard considered him the only real Santa. He carried a sack with presents. Each child had to recite a poem, then the gifts were handed out. Gerhard received a violin of ⅛ size. He loved it above all and began practising on it, at first playfully. In 1945 American soldiers stole this violin from within the body of the family's grandfather clock.

At Easter 1929 Gerhard was to be enrolled at school. At that time he wore his hair in a bob. Since this hairstyle would cause ridicule among his schoolmates, his mother took him first to a photographer and then to a hairdresser. There several of the locks that were cut off were gathered and tied with woollen strings to be given to relatives. Gerhard received a fringe hairstyle according to the fashion of that time, with hair only at the front, the back being shaved. Yet Gerhard's school enrolment in Rendsburg had to be called off since his father received his 'marching orders' for Stendal, where he was to take on the position of corps leader of the trumpet corps.

In the cavalry there was the staff sergeant (elsewhere sergeant), the cavalry captain (elsewhere captain), and the trumpet corps (military band). This band comprised only brass instruments and two kettledrums carried by an especially huge horse. The tympanist wore gauntlet gloves. Kettledrums are tuned to particular notes, while drums only produce sound. Ordinary military bands also include a woodwind section: clarinets and flutes. The cavalrymen used the derogatory term 'squeaky music' for this.

Gerhard's father had to master this new task without any preparation. He had to manage and conduct an orchestra without the appropriate training and to organise rehearsals. As if that was not enough, he also served as riding instructor. Trumpeters on horseback are not able to hold their reins and these were fixed at the height of the belt buckle. They also had to hold their instruments sideways, otherwise the horse might knock out their teeth with the instrument with a violent jerk of its head.

Military musicians were also coveted for weddings and other events. Only a few owned a telephone, so communication was through postcards.

The musicians returned late at night – around 2am – using their bicycles in any weather, their remuneration cash in their hands.

Thanks to this second income the military musicians were better off than other soldiers. A non-commissioned officer with a family had a monthly income of roughly 130 Marks in 1935. After the deduction of all household costs, around 20 Marks was left for the purchase of furniture or clothes. Therefore it was unfeasible that the child of a non-commissioned officer could attend a grammar school, since in addition to the expense of books one had to pay 20 Marks in school fees each month. A military musician, however, quite regularly had an additional income of around 120 Marks a month.

Gerhard's father mastered this challenge without difficulty as he possessed leadership qualities. He spent every evening at his desk and in waterproof ink wrote tunes into little music booklets, which were used while playing on horseback.

On 8 October 1929, Gerhard's Aunt Liesbet, his father's sister, married the non-commissioned officer Emil Reck, born in Upper Silesia, at Meiersberg. He served with Gerhard's father at Rendsburg. They celebrated at home, including dancing. Gerhard was asked to fetch his violin and he played 'Drink, drink, little brother, drink, leave your sorrows at home'. Late next morning the newlyweds entered the living room and took a seat on the sofa, not noticing that the violin was still lying there. The violin's top plate suffered three cracks and its neck was broken. It was not until Christmas 1935 that the repaired violin was returned to Gerhard, who was overjoyed. In addition, he received a beautiful bow, a reproduction of a specimen by the French bow maker Vuillaume, made from Pernambuco wood, which was the best as it was very light at 54g but exceedingly stiff, and also an elegant case.

Just like at Rendsburg, the family moved around until such time that they found the right apartment. An especially unpleasant task while changing apartments was the affixing of curtain tracks. For this long hooks had to be driven into the masonry. One had to look for mortar joints, as the stone bricks were too hard. Power drills and dowels had not been invented yet.

In Gerhard's recollection, Stendal was a beautiful town. There were four districts, each with a pretty brick church. Two churches, the cathedral and St Mary's, had two spires. The children learned in their local history lessons that the citizens took pride in raising the towers of St Mary's higher than those of the cathedral. A statue of Roland (a Frankish military leader under Charlemagne) stood on the market square in front of the town hall, allegedly the tallest of its kind. The town was surrounded by a rampart, which was still preserved in parts. Two well-preserved gates were the town's pride, and the Üngling Gate was especially impressive.

The Christmas market was held in the market square, the abbey church-yard and along the Brüdernstraße linking the two. There, Gustaf Nagel from Arendsee, known all over town, made his entrance, too. He was a peculiar person who worked as an itinerant preacher and natural healer. He wore a long robe similar to a night gown and sandals – just as one would imagine Jesus. Perhaps this was his intention. According to rumours, he allegedly dunked his children into cold water for such a long time during their baptism that some of them died because of this.

At Easter 1929, Gerhard was finally enrolled at school, which was close to the cathedral and very small. His teacher, Mr Stubbe, knew his father and learned from him that Gerhard could play the violin. Village and primary school teachers customarily played this instrument. During his first week Gerhard did not want to go to school and feigned belly aches.

At that time the Great Depression had reached its climax. Unemployment was extremely high, support minimal, and so abject poverty prevailed in many families. Therefore many suicides occurred during that period. It was noticeable that these were primarily carried out with gas and entire families were eradicated. In their neighbourhood a family man opened the gas valve and described the process, writing as long as he was able to still do so. His notoriety was achieved by this sentence: 'Hansi [their canary] is already dead.'

Stubbe and his family committed suicide by gas in 1931. His students were distributed among other schools and Gerhard was transferred to a large school in an entirely different district. One incident remained in his memory. Right at the beginning of a maths lesson a student was asked: 'What is four multiplied by six?' His answer was: 'Sixteen.' A string of other students were asked and they all repeated sixteen as if hypnotised, until it was Gerhard's turn and he answered undeterred: 'Twenty-four.' As a result he got to change his seat, as the best student had to sit in the back, the worst at the front.

At the edge of the town were the Petersburg Meadows, which were always flooded. During winter, ice skating took place there and the space was always very crowded. For the boys it was a kind of sport to steal the girls' student caps. At the end of the ice-covered surface, large ice blocks were sawn out of the ice sheet to be used by breweries. Farther away, the citizens' park was another day trip destination. The park was ideal for tobogganing and offered runs of varying difficulty, including the 'death run'. At that time children frequently played in the streets, mainly handball and dodge ball. Football was not popular yet. The smaller children played Cowboys and Indians. Gerhard's mother sewed trousers with fringes out of sackcloth for her children, and to this was added a red shirt and a hat with a very special dent – all this was very important.

Sometimes the children met along the railway tracks in order to see the rail Zeppelin, a futuristic-looking vehicle of aluminium and sailcloth powered by an aircraft engine with a propeller. It was invented in 1929 and from 1931 mainly travelled the Berlin–Hamburg route. At 230km/h, it held the world speed record for rail vehicles for twenty-five years. The children liked to place gun caps on the tracks, though their explosions could hardly be heard though the loud noise of the rail Zeppelin. Gerhard and his playmates were also interested in cars with their large spoke wheels, which only few people could afford during the years of economic depression.

Political education was not very developed then. Only very few owned a radio, not many more people could afford a daily newspaper. So one can well imagine that the masses were easily influenced by half-truths and lies. The causes for the rise of National Socialism lay in Hitler's charisma and rhetoric talent, and his sense for the things the Germans wanted to hear. He put his finger on the sore points: the Versailles Dictate (the peace treaty was only referred to in this way) and the miserable economic situation. The German people felt unutterably humiliated by this treaty, and Hitler blamed the Jews and democracy for the bad economic situation. Warnings by the Social Democrats that whoever voted for Hitler voted for war were sneered at.

Gerhard's parents belonged to a minority who were of a nationalist mind, but rejected Hitler and his NSDAP. Gerhard's conscious perception of his parents' attitude began 1930. He therefore viewed the developments during the Third Reich with some scepticism in contrast to the bulk of his schoolmates. As the majority of the youth were enamoured with the 'new times', he remained an outsider who did not feel as such. None of his classmates perceived him as a dissenter, since he took part in everything without being uptight.

Gerhard's moral commitment to his fatherland was a matter of course to him. This loyalty existed independently of the respective political leadership. If the fatherland was in danger, one had to fight for one's country, regardless of who was the ruler right then. So Gerhard always played along obediently, and performance of one's duty had the highest priority among all values.

At the beginning of the 1930s, all boys wore a kind of sports jacket and a lapel pin in the form of either a small swastika or three arrows according to the political views of their parents. The three arrows were the sign of the 'Iron Front', a coalition of the paramilitary organisation of the Social Democrats 'Black-Red-Gold Banner of the Realm' (*Reichsbanner Schwarz-Rot-Gold)* and other union-related and left groups, for example the Workers' Gymnastics Club. They had banded together in order to offer more effective resistance to the paramilitary organisation of the radical parties of the left and right, the SA([*Sturmabteilung* = Storm Troopers) and the Alliance of Red Front-Fighters (*Roter Frontkämpferbund*), who acted more and more violently. Yet in the end all this came to nothing: Hitler ascended to power in 1933.

On one occasion Gerhard witnessed a crying boy reaching his democratically disposed 'party comrades', who asked him immediately: 'Did the Nazis beat you up? Where are they?' Several boys who sympathised with the Nazis lived on that street. In one of the backyards they had a den reached by a ladder and Gerhard was taken along. A photo of Hitler from a newspaper was pinned to one of the walls. Rather solemnly, Gerhard was asked if he knew who this was. He nodded. As a result, at eight years old he became a probationary member. This was summer 1931. The other boys were three years older than him.

He has very vivid memories of the constant processions of the various parties. In his recollection there were four groups: the Communists, the Social Democrats, the Steel Helmet and the National Socialists. It was difficult to distinguish the Communists from the Social Democrats. His impression was that they had to appear for their processions in especially ragged clothes in order to demonstrate: we are miserable. In front were three women pushing shabby baby carriages, while behind them people with downturned mouths shuffled along. They stopped at the next corner, a speech was made and they sang the Internationale accompanied by shepherd's pipes. At the next square the same scene, the same speech.

The Steel Helmet were completely different: orderly, elderly gentlemen, former front-line fighters of the civil servant type, dressed neatly, more or less uniformly, but not rousing and rather proper. Again, the National Socialists were different: they also had a neat appearance, but there were more young faces in their ranks who gave the impression that the world was not that bad; they were of the optimistic student type. Regarding the many marches of the paramilitary organisations of the Weimar Republic, the National Socialist SA with their brown uniforms left the most determined impression.

Comparing the three groups, young Gerhard came to the following assessment: the Communists and Pinkos (Social Democrats) did not convey a positive vision of the future, while the Steel Helmet were solid but could they get Germany out of this mess? Probably not. The Nazis, yes, they radiated something positive, they would tackle the problem. And so Hitler gained more and more popularity, it was that simple. A duel shaped up: Communists versus National Socialists. Hitler won because he found support in national conservative circles and thus became acceptable to all who rejected the democratic system.

As a result Hitler was entrusted quite legally with the formation of a government on 30 January 1933. For most of the Germans this was no 'seizure of power'. The relevant political forces of the national conservative camp believed they would be able to master Hitler like a puppet, and looked upon him rather as a temporary solution en route to the resurrection of monarchy. Yet they picked the wrong person. How might they have rubbed their eyes in disbelief just eight weeks later when Hitler revealed his true face on 24 March 1933 with the Enabling Act! The real seizure of power.

The day after 30 January, Gerhard's class teacher Schmidt, a typical old front-line officer, nowadays with pince-nez and knickerbockers instead of a uniform, gave a brief speech in which he expressed his sympathies for Hitler: 'Now calm will return to our country, and everything will get better. Stand up, all of you, we will sing the national anthem.'

So the new times began. Shortly after, at Easter 1933, Gerhard experienced his next school transfer. Two students of his class of forty made it to grammar school. Lindhorst, whose parents owned a shop for wool and hence could afford to send their son there, and Gerhard. Their class teacher saw them both off. He wished Lindhorst all the best. To Gerhard he said: 'You'll probably make it.'

Because of his excellent grades Gerhard received a free place at the school, although his parents would have been able to pay for his place by now. School fees for middle school were 10 Marks a month, for grammar school 20 Marks, and external students also had to pay 25 Marks, since their parents did not pay taxes for the running of the school like the town residents. If several siblings attended the school, there was a sibling rebate of 10 Marks. This rule from the Weimar Republic was kept during the Third Reich.

In Stendal Gerhard attended the Classical Languages Grammar School because there was no other. It was supposedly among the ten oldest schools in Germany and had previously been a Latin school for monks. Fittingly it was located in the abbey churchyard. Until 1935 all middle and grammar school students wore student caps. At some schools each grade had a different colour for the entire cap, but most of the time there were only different colours of ribbons for the caps when advancing. When a change of class was near at Easter, the milliner was very busy. The boys had caps with peaks, the girls caps without them. Girls whose schools sported peaked caps considered themselves to be very chic.

At the grammar school the grades were given Latin names, counting backward from *Sexta*, *Quinta*, *Quarta* to *Prima*, the final grade. Also, the elementary schools had a decremental system starting with the eighth grade. This was only changed with the new naming of grammar schools: in the Third Reich from 1938 onward they were known as higher schools for boys or girls respectively. There the grades started at one. Only classical languages schools kept their old name (Gymnasium).

During *Sexta* Gerhard Ehlert was sitting next to a boy called Herbert Kath. His father was a railway worker and he lived in Karnipp, an area where poorer people lived. He had a free place, too. The two of them became friends. For Gerhard's birthday he gave him a copy of *Münchhausen's Adventures*, bought at the EPA for 25 Pfennigs. EPA (Einheitspreis AG = Standard Price Corporation) only sold items at 10, 25, 50, 75 or 100 Pfennigs. It was a large department store where during winter many people visited just to be warm. Herbert Kath met Gerhard Ehlert again in 1945 in captivity.

At ten years old Gerhard received violin lessons from bandmaster Schulze for two Marks an hour. He now played a ¾-size violin that he had borrowed from his cousin Erich Zunk. His skills were good enough for him to play second violin in the school orchestra. The first piece he performed with it was Mozart's *The Abduction from the Seraglio*, although he had no idea what the lyrics meant. The weekly rehearsals took place in the auditorium. Every Monday began with a morning service held by the teachers.

At the start of grammar school, everybody joined the junior organisation of the Hitler Youth except Gerhard. His parents forbade it. This was an organisation for ten to fourteen-year-olds within the Hitler Youth. Gerhard only joined on 2 May 1934. There was no political education in the junior organisation or at school, and that was the case for all towns where the Ehlert family moved.

At the barracks where Ehlert's father served, traditional festivals were celebrated regularly. Veterans who had in part served even before the First World War came as old-timers. These were almost exclusively farmer's sons used to handling horses. The officers came from the rural nobility of the Mark Brandenburg and sometimes attended with their wives. Mentally they were still living in the monarchy, and their mode of expression matched this. The simple soldiers came with their women, the non-commissioned officers with their wives, and the officers with their ladies, as was proper. Lower ranks and non-commissioned officers were asked: 'Where did you serve?' The question to officers was: 'Where did you stand?'

There were still many uniforms from the imperial era for military branches that no longer existed: cuirassiers, dragoons, lancers and hussars. The small Reichswehr with its 100,000 men maintained the tradition of the old army. Each squadron took on the tradition of a regiment. Quadrilles were ridden, always in old uniforms. Food was provided by a field kitchen, of course, and it was always a very social gathering: do you still remember the old times?

For Gerhard the autumn hunts were always exciting. There were three of them: St Hubert's chase, a fox hunt and one other. For the fox hunt the victor of the previous year kept the fox tail at home. He fastened the tail to his shoulder, loose enough that the uniform was not damaged when it was torn off. He got a head start, then all the riders, perhaps 150, chased after him in order to tear off the tail. On the hunting grounds the field kitchen provided pea soup, everybody received a twig of oak leaves, a group picture was taken, and then they headed back to the barracks through the town and accompanied by music. All family members were driven in horse-drawn carriages – a great spectacle. Gerhard tried to be at the barracks before the huntsmen as he had friends among the soldiers, onto whose horses he was allowed to climb once they had ridden through the gate. At one occasion there was nearly a serious accident. When the horse he was riding turned onto the straight road leading to the stable, the nag probably smelled home and immediately went into a gallop. Gerhard clung to the saddle, he saw the stable door and sensed it was too low, so he bent onto the horse as flat as possible. They entered the stable at full speed, whereupon the horse rushed into its box and came to a halt. Gerhard heaved a sigh of relief.

The political change began without being noticed by many. The critical opponents of Hitler, however, perceived even the tiniest alterations. When Storm Troopers stood in front of Jewish shops to deter customers, this was accepted without thinking. People were indoctrinated daily in political speeches that the Jews were their doom. In 1933 the first concentration camp was established at Dachau – in the opinion of many a kind of labour camp or reformatory, nothing more. On 30 June and 1 July 1934 the 'Röhm putsch' took place. Hitler believed that Ernst Röhm, the SA's leader, might turn his organisation into a people's army, a rival for the Reichswehr on which Hitler relied. Live ammunition was distributed among Reichswehr soldiers, just in case. Gerhard had observed this at the barracks. In a cloak-and-dagger operation, Hitler had Röhm and all the other people out of favour, among them the former Reich chancellor General Schleicher and his wife, murdered by members of the SS, a new paramilitary party organisation – indiscriminately and without trial.

A year later a tragic death occurred in the Ehlert family: Gerhard's brother Konrad died on 9 June 1935 due to kidney failure. His father came to his school during lessons and informed his second son. For Gerhard this was inconceivable; he could not cope with the death of his brother. The family drove in the car carrying the coffin to Meiersberg, where Konrad was buried. He was displayed in the open coffin in his grandparents' living room. His grandparents drew the curtains and covered the mirror with a cloth.

For Gerhard, the sight of his dead brother was as eerie as the fact that a burial site for three people was established at Meiersberg: in the middle the one for Konrad, the other two for his parents, who planned to spend their retirement in the town. For the first time in his life Gerhard had to face up to death, which he only encountered again late during the war when the professor bled out in the doomed Do 217.

Ehlert is lying on his bunk staring at the ceiling. He tries to put the dismal memories out of his mind. He wants to think of more pleasant matters than death. For example, of how much he enjoyed eating green herring as a boy. When the fisherman was in the village, Gerhard cycled to all his relatives living there. He knocked at all six doors and asked whether there was green herring for lunch in order to invite himself along for this meal. Ehlert fancies having its taste on his tongue and recalls further delicacies.

At that time blueberries were abundant in the forest, called *Bäsing* in the local dialect. Many villagers went *Bäsing* picking to earn money. One pound could be sold for 5 to 12 Pfennigs. During wet summers there were many blueberries, albeit they were quite watery. These yielded only 5 Pfennigs.

In summer 1934 Ehlert had a new goal. He needed 14 Mark to buy pho-tographic equipment: a Balda box camera for 6 Mark, and in addition a bag, tripod, a cable release and delayed-action shutter release. It took him three weeks to earn the money. He immediately started to take pictures: Aunt Meta churning butter, Aunt Erna milking the cows, other relatives harvesting rye with scythes and binding it to sheaves, finally a group photo after the harvest. So he did not take pictures indiscriminately, as they cost money, he asked himself before each one: would you stick this picture into your album? A good control measure.

A special sound also belonged to Meiersberg that resulted from the sharpening of the scythes. During this process the scythe blades were beaten flat with a scythe hammer on a scythe anvil and thus sharpened. A scythe anvil consisted of a slightly convex iron sheet measuring 5cm × 5cm on top of a chopping block. To place the scythe blades at the correct inclination onto the scythe anvil, a rope was tied to the scythe stick or handle and a stone fixed to its bottom end. The rope was placed across a thick branch in such a manner that everything was well balanced.

At some point during summer 1935 Gerhard got his hands on an air pistol, with which he shot holes into the weathervane of the neighbouring barn. One of his playmates at that time was Arno Meier, as Ehlert recalls clearly. Together they went to the carpenter Max Ehlert, who was a distant relative of Gerhard, and one of the most successful poachers in the whole region to boot. The boys asked him to make them a blowpipe: the internal diameter was 8mm, the external 28mm and it was 110cm long. It was made from two parts, into each of which a semicircular groove had been sliced. Glued together they made up the blowpipe. A mouthpiece was whittled resembling that of a trumpet. The pipe started off octagonally at the mouthpiece and at 30cm became circular. Finally, the pipe was stained red brown. It cost 80 Pfennig. Max Ehlert apologised for the high price, since in 1910 it had only cost 50 Pfennig, yet the two boys did not mind.

They shot with so-called 'puffers'. These were made from three layers of 5cm × 5cm linen squares. Apart from a small bit, these were made to fray and stuck onto a nail, bent double, tied together with sewing thread and cropped neatly with scissors. The nail was whetted by file. With these one could perform target shooting at wooden discs at a distance of 10m.

Ehlert smiles at the ceiling of his dorm. He believes himself far away from war and captivity, when he thinks of that time. And yet his thoughts wander back to the crux, effectively the zero hour of his life, to the moment when he chose Nazi Germany and the Luftwaffe. Or was there no such moment? Was it really a gradual process?

He remembers the important events of his youth such as 20 April 1937, when on the 'Leader's Birthday' his cohort graduated from the junior organisation to the actual Hitler Youth. This was combined with a great celebration that took place at dusk. During the procession to the venue, a low mountain on which a Bismarck monument stood, the boys on the outside carried torches. All the boys formed a large square, in the centre of which a huge fire was burning. Pithy phrases were uttered, and Gerhard was deeply impressed. Was it that evening that has brought him here, into the prison camp at Yelabuga?

Probably not, Ehlert thinks. He would still have had the opportunity to dodge the whole matter, to follow his parents and especially his mother, who had always warned her sons of the 'devil in disguise' as soon as the conversation turned to Hitler and his party. Therefore it must have been an another instance. There must have been a watershed after which there was no turning back.

Ehlert reflects. He recalls the time when he was called up for military service. In spring 1940, half a year before the start of his duty, he had to go to an examination in Hanover at the second receiving office for Luftwaffe cadets. This examination was the most important and the most difficult, as he learned later. Only a third were accepted.

After a medical examination the candidates had to sit down on a chair. The first aptitude test went as follows: the hands and face were covered with cloths so that no draft of air could touch the skin. Now the chair was slowly turned. The candidate had to tell in which direction he was being turned. This was no problem for young Ehlert. He also mastered the second test for speed of reaction without difficulty. Five plates of 15cm ×15 cm were placed next to each other on a rectangular box. One was marked in red, one in blue, a circle was painted on the third, a square on the fourth and a dot on the last. The room was blacked out. Then the five signs appeared at irregular intervals on a screen. Fixed to the box were five levers corresponding to the signs that had to be pulled whenever the respective sign appeared on the screen. This was accompanied by a simultaneous acoustic test. One had to push the left foot pedal when one heard a deep hum, and the right pedal at another sound. Three hundred signs were shown. Then all the signs were shuffled, and the test resumed.

Ehlert passed with flying colours, yet he was not done yet. He had to learn a long text by rote before a gymnastic exercise and this had to be recited afterwards. The candidates had also been informed that they would have to give a presentation, so they prepared their topics. When the young men were finally called forward, they stood in front of an audience of fifteen people – and were suddenly confronted with an entirely different topic than previously agreed upon. The candidates had to speak full sentences and were closely observed by a psychologist. The latter cross-examined each individual candidate together with other examiners and tried to trip up the young men. He asked manipulative questions regarding order and discipline, which prompted the candidates to talk in glowing terms of their neat desks at home. A few minutes and questions later their desk at home was the topic of conversation again, but now from a creative perspective. And many candidates simply changed their opinion. Now their desk was a chaotic treasure trove of wild creativity.

Be on your guard, Gerhard thought to himself, and stuck to his description of order on his desk. During the conversation, during which the examiners took rapid turns to ask questions that had to be answered just as promptly, the psychologist asked the candidates to put two spheres on the table in front of them on top of each other. Whoever even touched the metal spheres after that was out – likewise the candidate who took off his jacket because he found the room in which the psychological exam took place too stifling. Laxness was not in demand with the officers' acceptance process of the Luftwaffe. The procedure lasted for three days in total. Gerhard passed on 22 July 1940, and he still feels the elation today. It was his first step towards pilot training.

Ehlert received his draft call for 15 October 1940 with the 3rd Company of Trainee Aviator Battalion 16 in Schleswig. France had been defeated, the Luftwaffe was bombing British towns and cities, and allied Italy attacked Greece in an overestimation of its abilities – a fatal move that would entangle Germany in a campaign in the Balkans, finally resulting in the German attack on the Soviet Union in summer 1941 being postponed for weeks. This delay was the reason that the Wehrmacht did not reach Moscow before the onset of winter – possibly a turn decisive in the outcome of the war.

Great events often come from little causes, Ehlert thinks on his bunk in Yelabuga. He vividly remembers that time scarcely five years ago. Half of his class wanted to become officers at all costs then. For the accepted cadets, 5 October 1940 was their last day in school, while the others stayed until 1941 and sat the usual exams for their A-levels. On that day Ehlert and his classmates went in their Sunday best with their class teacher Dr Gustaf Wüster to the photographer Blankenhorn for a final class photo. Then the young men strolled together to the *Ratskeller* (the name for any bar or restaurant located in the basement of the town hall or nearby) for a cosy farewell celebration. Ehlert's classmate Dieter Wustrau, who wished to join the navy, took a cigar case from his breast pocket, chose a cigar, cut its tip and began to smoke. Dr Wüster took note of it with a smile. The mood was not sad, as one might have expected on such a day. It was a normal farewell. Once again Ehlert calls the class photo to mind now. More than half of the young men will have fallen by May 1945. On the morning of 14 October 1940 Ehlert's father accompanied his son to the train station. At their farewell he said by way of consolation: 'The bullet is not cast for everyone, my son.'

Even though he was slightly nervous, Ehlert looked forward to Schleswig and basic training. First he wanted to leave his suitcases somewhere and explore the town. Yet it was to be different. Myriad young men alighted from the train that day. At the station stood soldiers holding signs with different units written on them. Ehlert queued for the 3rd Company of the 16th Trainee Aviator Battalion, then he and the others marched to the barracks at the River Schlei. Sightseeing had to wait.

Inside the barracks, the new soldiers immediately received their uniforms. Then they were divided into groups of ten men and platoons of thirty. After the first four weeks in Schleswig, Ehlert's company commander had to attest to his school in Göttingen that he, Gerhard Ehlert, was now a soldier. That meant that he was sent his school leaving certificate. Ehlert thus had his A-levels in the bag without sitting a single exam. His wartime A-levels, as well as all A-level certificates until 1942, were recognised for eligibility for university entrance, while all those issued later had to be repeated. The reasoning: because of the many air raid alarms since 1942 it had not been possible to teach adequate lessons. Ehlert was lucky once again.

Ehlert shared a dorm with the men of his group. Each had a narrow locker, while the beds were bunks. The duvet consisted of a wool blanket in a cover, which had to be folded extremely neatly. Every day a different man had dorm cleaning duty. During evening roll call at the dorm a speck of dust was always found somewhere – on top of a locker or inside a power outlet. Basic training took three months: marching, saluting, shooting with carbine, pistol and machine gun. A song was sung when they marched to their mess hall.

The young soldiers were 'honed' at intervals. That meant they were drilled to the limits of their capacity, sometimes ending in the wash room where they had to do squats wearing their gas masks and holding their rifles in their extended arms. Ehlert and his comrades considered suchlike complete nonsense. This had nothing to do with rational training. In each group was an officer candidate, recognisable from afar by an armband around the left upper arm. Ehlert's platoon leader at that time was an older Unteroffizier from Ducherow, 15km away from Meiersberg, a quiet, calm person, not the drill sergeant type. One evening he took Ehlert aside and smirked: 'You'll become a general one day.'

The 'general' is now lying on his bunk in the prison camp at Yelabuga and has only managed to become a Leutnant Ehlert reflects. For the first time he has the sense that the war has taken something from him. He becomes impatient, but quickly pushes away those thoughts again and remembers his training, which after the basics continued for another six weeks in Schleswig. Ehlert had to take the so-called non-commissioned course, which was actually only a continuation of basic training. At the end he and his fellow cadets were officially appointed cadets (as a rank). This made hardly any change to their uniform: a thin, round silver cord was fixed to their shoulder boards.

Training at the flight school in Werder near Potsdam began at the beginning of March with theoretical lessons in navigation, radio communication, engine studies, fluid mechanics, meteorology and so on. On 16 April 1941, a Wednesday, Ehlert had his first familiarisation flight in a Bücker Bü 131 Jungmann biplane. On 17 May, after eighty-three flights – five-minute circuits with flight instructors – he was considered capable of undertaking a solo flight. He recalled what an exciting affair that was, even though nothing ever happened as a rule because the young pilots were overly cautious.

Take-off and landing took place next to the so-called landing cross. This was no cross, but a large T-shape of white cloth. The vertical and horizontal part each measured 10m × 1m. The goal was to take off and land as closely as possible on the right side of the horizontal part. After the first thirty circuits flown solo they had to perform emergency landing exercises with a flight instructor. For this the instructor suddenly pulled the throttle into an idle state and thus simulated an engine failure. The trainee pilot now had to immediately look for a spot in the terrain suitable for landing. Then a mock landing was performed down to a few metres above ground, and finally they pulled up again at full throttle.

The cross-country flights of that time stayed in Ehlert's mind as a particular diversion. For those he had to calculate the compass course. On the map the direction was measured with a course triangle, then three influences on the compass course were taken into account: wind, magnetic deviation due to the metal parts of the plane and the constantly changing location of the magnetic north. The aviation maps were 1:300,000 scale, the principal reference points in nature were forests and water, which were highlighted in colour. Sometimes one lost one's orientation. In aviator slang that meant *sich verfranzen* (to lose one's way). Then one left the prescribed altitude against orders – you were not allowed to go lower than 300m – and flew along a railway. The rough guide was: left wheel (of the plane), right track. When a train station came in sight, one flew so low that one could read the sign with the place name.

The destinations of Ehlert's flight school were Magdeburg, Stendal, Hanover, Erfurt, Pyritz, Neubrandenburg, Szczecin, Strausberg, and Prenzlau. On external airfields one had to report to air traffic control. Then the aircraft was refuelled. Most training aircraft at that time only held enough fuel for three hours.

Once a month a special ritual was held for all Luftwaffe pilots and those aspiring to be such. They had to fall in for a roll call wearing their steel helmets. Then an officer read out Paragraph 92 concerning aviation discipline and order. For Ehlert and his comrades this ritual became a diverting, amusing affair because after the paragraph had been recited like a mantra, all the aviation-related offences committed inside the German Reich during the last month were described in detail. The young pilots were amazed at the pranks some of their colleagues had played in high jinks. One simply landed on a meadow near his home village, another circled the village church spire at low altitude. Yet another flew daringly below a bridge. None of this was permitted and the punishment for such a lack of discipline was quite varied: it ranged from six months detention to being stripped of one's rank.

In August 1941, when the Wehrmacht had already been heading for Moscow for six weeks and one success story followed the next, Ehlert's unit was transferred to an airfield east of Magdeburg. There the young pilots undertook their training for five weeks. The first night flights were scheduled, albeit just traffic circuits.

The supervising officer at that time was Wolf-Dieter Dahinden. The senior lieutenant wounded during the French campaign had a stiff elbow joint and had been awarded the Iron Cross First Class. He left a deep impression on the young aviators with his personality, his appearance and his voice.

In Magdeburg he was living with his young wife Ilse outside the barracks. One balmy evening the trainee aviators and their supervising officer met for a convivial gathering where alcohol was flowing copiously. Ehlert took his box gramophone along, which he had bought in Berlin. One of the men had provided some humorous sheets with texts and drawings. One drawing showed a low-wing aircraft. In its back seat sat their supervising officer, before him his wife, her scarf flying. The plane bore the marking WD + Ilse. Dahinden had indeed made a circuit with his wife against regulations.

Recalling this, Ehlert is smiling to himself while lying on his bunk. And he recalls a flight that nearly cost him his head. One day after his nineteenth birthday he was supposed to fly home another supervising officer, Bressel, another of his instructors. Bressel had quit the service at Werder and wanted to join the front-line troops. The two pilots took a French Caudron C.440, a spacious twin-engine liaison aircraft, because they had to transport furniture, too. Ehlert was joined by a second pilot and a radio operator. Their destination was Stolp in Eastern Pomerania, but beforehand the pilot was supposed to land on a meadow at Groß Tychow where Bressel wanted to unload his furniture. Bressel's father was the head forester there.

Ehlert did not know if this stopover had been permitted, but did not bother himself with the formalities. Trainee pilots like him were only allowed to fly half an hour after sunrise and half an hour before sunset. As there was some damage to the aircraft, their take-off was delayed. Finally they started at 4:30pm, and this made it inevitable that Ehlert would land in Stolp during darkness. As a flight instructor, Bressel was his superior. Should he refuse?

The aircraft flew south around Berlin, as the capital was a no-fly area. Then they continued toward Groß Tychow. South-east of Szczecin, Ehlert saw the sun set above Lake Miedwie (Madü). They landed at Groß Tychow at around 5:40pm, where a cart to transport the furniture had been waiting on the meadow since lunchtime. When Ehlert was about to take off again, Bressel changed their plan: 'Do not fly to Stolp, but to Kolobrzeg [Kolberg], that is closer.' Ehlert took the map and determined the compass course and their flight time. He realised instantly that this last-minute change of plan was the wrong decision. Their flight was not registered in Kolobrzeg and the flight time was only six minutes shorter in total.

Nevertheless, the young pilot obeyed and took off in the gathering dark. He flew into the night. According to the flight time calculated, he should have reached Kolobrzeg soon after, but he simply could not spot anything on the ground. The night was extremely dark, so Ehlert decided to do an about-turn, as he suspected that he was already flying over the Baltic Sea. He flew exactly the same route back and hoped to be able to spot the coast line through close observation. Since the radio was broken to boot, the men inside the plane were in dire straits. In any case, Ehlert could not land in the dark. There remained only one option: to gain altitude and take to their parachutes – an extremely unpleasant measure since they did not know the outcome of this manoeuvre. Hopefully the plane would crash into some field and not any habitation. However, rescue came at the very last moment. Once again Ehlert remained lucky. He had calculated his course so exactly that he flew right over the Kolobrzeg airfield on his return. Exactly at that minute the airfield commenced night-time operations. The airfield beacons were switched on, and everything suddenly went bright.

Ehlert did one more circuit to discern their direction for landing, then he commenced landing procedures. When he had reached an altitude of just 20m, a gigantic black shadow passed over his aircraft. It was a Ju 52, the standard transport plane of the Luftwaffe, likewise trying to land. Its pilot spotted the small aircraft and pulled up at the last second. Ehlert's blood ran cold. Nevertheless, he focussed on landing and this proceeded without hitch. He rolled his small aircraft as far out as possible in order to avoid further air traffic.

When Ehlert and the two others had alighted, they experienced a decidedly hostile reception and were taken to the head of the pilot school. The latter treated the three as if they had committed a crime. The next day they had to travel back to Werder by train, the plane remaining at Kolobrzeg. Court martial proceedings were opened against Ehlert because of his prohibited night landing, but were later abandoned when he was deployed to the front.

Ehlert's time at the war college in Werder was mainly filled by flight duty. Preparation for an officer's career was restricted to inconsequential etiquette. The commander of the war college, Count Luckner, a cousin of the renowned 'sea devil' famous for his extravagant naval warfare during the First World War, showed the young officers how to negotiate a ceremonial gala dinner. The supervising officer further instructed them on how to conduct a proper introduction. His young wife assisted him in this. While soldiers were dying before Moscow, the young German trainee pilots practised the correct kiss on the hand. Ehlert and his comrades even received lessons in sabre fencing, but never had the opportunity to prove their skill in a real-life scenario.

Weeks and months passed without the pilots ever facing an enemy, during which one training flight after another had to be performed. It took time until Ehlert was finally introduced to his actual field of application, long-range reconnaissance. The main task of this additional training was to photograph correctly. The long-range reconnaissance trainees flew at low altitude along the River Elbe while the camera release had to be fired at the right moment. In addition, Ehlert had to learn to analyse the photographs. Why, he is now asking himself. After all, this was always done by the specialists, us pilots actually never did this.

After completing this training, another selection was made: most became day-time long-range reconnaissance pilots, and better pilots naval reconnaissance aviators. The best, however, became night-time long-range reconnaissance pilots. Ehlert was actually no overachiever, but had a mathematical talent. Perhaps this was the reason why he was deployed to the last group. Once again he underwent rigorous training, this time with the 4th Night-Time Long-Range Reconnaissance Group. When Ehlert arrived for his training there, it was stationed close to a village near Brzeg (Brieg) in Silesia. Frederick II of Prussia had fought his first battle not far away.

There they flew exclusively at night. As Ehlert remembers, this was much more exciting than during the day. In principle night pilots had two options for orientation: when there was enough light the reconnaissance pilots flew at low altitudes up to 400m along roads and railway tracks – just like the night they were shot down and the professor and Schlotter died. The second option was to fly by radio. Germany possessed a network of radio beacons that transmitted female first names with four letters: Ilse, Inge, Anna – all in Morse code.

Training focussed on two areas: reconnaissance by eye and photography with a flashlight. To complete their training, Ehlert and his comrades had to perform so-called night navigation flights – the absolute highlight of aviation. Fog was simulated during take-off, then they ascended to 3,000m, flew over Poland for four hours with course changes every ten minutes, and had to know where they were at all times. Wind predictions and ground speed checks were carried out during the flight. An unknown airfield was approached and they performed a blind landing manoeuvre there. If they encountered a freight train, a flare was to be set off in order to take note of its cargo.

After this intensive training, Ehlert was deployed to the front in autumn 1943. For night-time long-range reconnaissance in Russia a squadron of thirteen to fifteen crews each was slated for each section of the front – North, Centre or South. Ehlert ended up at Army Group Centre, where the pressure of the Russians on the German front line, or what remained of it, would be the highest. He flew sortie after sortie, even when his faith in a final victory had already been extinguished. Until that day when he and his crew were shot down he had functioned like a machine. And now, on 8 May 1945, the day of the German surrender, which he spends in the Yelabuga camp, he knows that he has lost many years of his life. The long period of his training – all in vain. And outweighing this: his internal compass no longer shows any direction, either. What will be next? Will he ever see his home again and hold Riele in his arms?

7

Freezing Hell

Yelabuga, one day after the end of war. The entire camp has to fall in for muster. The Russians announce loudly that the war is over. From now on new rules apply: now the officers of the German and Japanese armies up to the rank of captain must also work. And now is the time to eat less. The outward appearance of the prisoners will change completely, too. Rank insignia, uniforms, medals etc vanish. The captives gradually turn into a uniformly grey mass in which the individual drowns.

Ehlert and his fellow officers are hit with hard work right from the start. The few Panje horses for supplying the camp have died during the winter due to an epidemic. Tractors or trucks have been gobbled up by the front. Therefore the young German officers are now turned into draught animals. At 5am they are woken, they fetch bread and wait for the call to their morning soup. With their soup they eat their entire daily ration of bread so that they feel sated at least once a day. Day by day their cultural programme, reading and education becomes more and more inconceivable. The Russians suddenly no longer treat the Germans as prisoners of war, but like convicts. Time and again, larger details have to be deployed for tasks around the camp. Many work for a construction trust. The civilian personnel whom the German captives encounter in the stone pits, at the lime kiln and the brickworks consist largely of recently released Soviet convicts. In their dealings with them, the Germans learn scanty but serviceable Russian. They are standing naked among naked – not only during the 'meat inspection' carried out each month by the commission assessing their fitness for work, consisting of the Soviet camp commander, his deputy and a female doctor of the NKVD. The latter pinches one prisoner after another in his bottom in a bored manner, in order to assess with a practised grip for which type of work he is suited – a deeply humiliating procedure that reminds Ehlert of slave markets of the distant past.

In Yelabuga the mood of both the prisoners and of the guards deteriorates week by week. And yet, it will get much worse still. In November 1945 the emaciated former German pilot, shaking with cold even in mild autumn temperatures, is transferred to the forest camp of Bolshoy Bor. There he is supposed to log and transport trees with other prisoners. The camp is located in the middle of the forest and there is not a drop of water in the vicinity. Water for the daily soup is fetched by a sleigh crew from the village 3½km away and the trip has to be made twice a day.

Meanwhile, out in nature it has become painfully cold. The first snow is falling. Ehlert and his fellow captives slosh through the mud and sleet and are glad when they are allowed to vanish into their barely heated earth bunkers. Here below ground, it is already much warmer than outside. The onset of the Russian winter hampers their work as a matter of course. The timber they have to transport is covered in snow and ice. Sometimes a trunk slips from one's hand and falls onto a neighbour's legs. Then screams, insults and cursing can be heard.

The slipping of an iced trunk is also the cause of one comrade's fatal fall into a gorge. The dead will never be found again. In Ehlert's camp, during the following weeks some comrades will die because of severe illness or malnutrition. As there is no cemetery, the dead are simply lain in the forest next to the camp. No cross, not even a modest sign, marks their cold graves. The mounting snow covers the dead and they become untraceable. When one day a Russian commission arrives to record how many German captives have died, the guards quickly dig several pits, fill them with stones and cover them with snow and soil. The Russians develop a lively imagination when it comes to false reports to their superior authorities.

Day after day Ehlert and his comrades pursue their labour while hungry and exhausted. When it is snowy and icy the timber is transported by sleighs, otherwise it is carried in two-wheel carts. Six men pull, and another walks next to the sleigh to prevent it overturning. More and more political prisoners arrive at the camp. The approximately 200 men break down into various groups, whose fate is quite different. Aside from camp command and a few doctors, the kitchen crew and the craftsmen whetting the saws and axes are able to make somewhat bearable arrangements for themselves. Fifteen men cut down the trees. They enjoy certain privileges, too. And then there is the large bunch of deplorables who have to pull the sleighs. Ehlert is among them. Most of them stay in an earth bunker with two entrances. Two small stoves provide the scant warmth that keeps the prisoners alive. It is dark inside the bunkers, dim even during the day. The Russian guard details live outside the camp. Yet for these young people, the solitude in which they live next to the forest camp is punishment, too.

In the morning Ehlert and the others wait for the sleigh details to be called up. It is still dark and the snow only emanates a faint glow when they fetch their sleighs and get ready on the camp street. The men check the self-made pulling devices. About a third of the sleighs have good pulling devices in the form of ropes and hemp loops for grip. The others only have a wire for pulling attached. Of course, they cannot pull on the wire without injuring themselves so sticks are fixed to it. Two men of the same height pull at each side of a stick, which is between the belly button and groin. In addition, each prisoner has a so-called 'biter', a wooden implement 1.70m long resembling a crowbar. The timber is moved around using this.

The men are forced to wait until the sleigh unit is ready to set out. During this period they feel the biting cold the most, making any conversation impossible. At least Ehlert has obtained a pair of worn and mended Red Army felt boots in the meantime. In the low shoes he got from the Siberian at the command post soon after his capture he would quickly suffer from the worst frostbite here – like so many of his army comrades. Some of them are still wearing the accursed leather boots to which they owed much frostbite during the winters during the war.

At dawn the sleigh convoy starts to move. On days when the Buran – the Russian winter storm – blows and drives the snow in a flurry in front itself, only the prisoners' heads are visible. They are bundled up beyond all recognition, wear self-made nose guards, and still uncovered or inadequately protected spots on face and hands suffer from frostbite. Only rubbing them in snow helps, Ehlert has learned.

The timber cut down the day before is often left lying off the track. Of course, it is not neatly stacked so the transport details have to look for it under the snow and ice. Then they have to dig out the 2m trunks from the snow. This results in dangerously cold hands. Yet the daily norm they have to load is one solid cubic metre, i.e. around 800kg per head, which means over 100kg of tensile load. The return journey takes time and strength. None of the routes are level, heights and dips have to be overcome, snow drifts make the transport difficult, their cargo slips out of position, and sleighs overturn. A day's march of 30km is no problem for a well-fed soldier. He has victuals in his haversack and tea in his canteen, while the field kitchen provides him with a nourishing stew. Yet even the hardiest wanderer will not get through such a day without rest and not without shelter during winter.

And Ehlert? None of the 'draught cattle' still has his normal body weight, including the pilot. In the camp kitchen, the Soviet functionaries help themselves first, then the emigrants follow, old Communists from Germany who are supposed to free the captives from National Socialist ideology, tempting them with double rations to join the anti-fascist movement. Camp command, cultural brigade, kitchen and mess hall details, bread cutters, bakers, plumbers, locksmiths, hairdressers, medics, doctors – all help themselves from the camp provisions at the remaining prisoners' cost.

One evening, one of the sleigh details is supposed to pull long timber to a shipyard. On the sleigh lies a huge 12m-long tree trunk, the end of which is mounted to a smaller sleigh at the very back. There is a thick flurry of snow. Nevertheless, Ehlert and the other thirteen men have to go out into the deadly cold. The weather is still quite calm in the forest itself, yet as soon as the men reach the fields the flurry of snow turns into a storm. Snowflakes pierce the men's faces like pins and needles. They are used to this though. The particular problem they face, however, is that the road has been drifted over by the snow storm and can no longer be found. Dusk is followed by darkness within minutes. For 3km the men pull the tree trunk through the deepest snow. Again and again they sink hip-deep into snow drifts – an undue exertion for the underfed men that drives tears of rage and desperation into the eyes of some. At some point two of the prisoners collapse and cannot be induced to get up again and use their last strength for the tree transport, even by persuasion. Ehlert and the others have to leave them behind in order not to risk their own lives. On their return journey they intend to pick the men up again. Yet their return becomes a funeral procession. The two men remain lost without trace. At night the totally exhausted men return to their bunks in the sparsely heated bunkers. And all of them know: if their guards released them into freedom now, they would beg to stay in the camp.

Then another Christmas comes around, one that has nothing in common with the wonderful celebration at Yelabuga. The prisoners of war hardly take notice. Everybody knows that it is Christmas Eve, but their mood is sullen. Ehlert is lying next to his comrades in the hardly heated bunker and all kinds of thoughts go through his mind: Shall he say a few words about this day? Shall he simply start to sing 'Silent Night'? The comrades would most probably join in, even if only hesitatingly at the beginning. Yet he has no longer enough courage for this.

Week after week passes in the new year of 1946. Out into the forest, work, eat, sleep. Always the same rhythm of prisoner life accompanied by hunger and depression, which is briefly alleviated for some by the first mail from home. The deadly rhythm, however, catches up fast with all of them.

Ehlert hopes to get rid of this constant pressure through a short break, a little holiday from his labour in the forest. If only he could get duty inside the camp! If only he could perform lighter tasks for a short while due to his state of health! Yet how could this come about? He develops an idea. The moment for what he has planned for days seems now opportune. For the final time that day he and his comrades are putting a timber on the sleigh, and since their march back takes place without a snow storm and in relatively mild temperatures, they reach the camp quite early and hence also the end of their shift. Ehlert knows that this is the only moment to act unnoticed. Therefore he slowly lets his comrades pass him in front of the camp gate while pretending that he is taking a short rest.

After a few minutes he is suddenly all alone. He looks for the sharp stone that he has hidden days earlier at the roadside and digs it from the snow. He is fully resolved and with all his might he drops the stone onto his foot. He could just scream, but bites his tongue. The pain drives tears into his eyes. He drops the stone onto his foot two or three times, after all the injury is to buy him a few days in the sick bay. Suddenly however, he has qualms about the righteousness of his attempt. At first these are less moral reservations than the consideration of what might happen if the Russians do not buy his story about the accident. If even the Wehrmacht shot soldiers during the war for self-mutilation, one cannot fathom the consequences here. He puts the stone aside. Gloomily he stirs himself and limps towards the camp gate in agony. There he notices in astonishment that no guard post is waiting for him. And inside his earth bunker nobody is expecting him, either. All have already lain down and are fast asleep. He lies down on his bunk, and everything around him is peaceful. His foot throbs a little, but can be moved freely. Nothing seems to be broken. The easing pain and the warmth of his sleeping comrades stir a blissful feeling inside Ehlert, and he is grateful that he has not gone through with his plan after all.

If they do not work, the men lie like sardines inside the earth bunkers day in and day out. The bunk beds are divided into sections assigned to seven men each, on which they have to lie together so closely that they have to spoon. If just one of them wants to turn around, he wakes the other six. Since the gap between the bunks and the wall is merely half a metre wide, only three of the fourteen men in total (top and bottom bunk) can dress and undress themselves while standing. The other have to do so sitting or lying down. Among the worst strains on the prisoners is the fact that they are never able to be on their own inside the camp, even for the most private matters. This might be the reason why those who survive will later avoid all large congregations of people. On the other hand, Ehlert feels that during those days the forced cohabitation at close quarters does not have only negative aspects. They learn to be more tolerant, to be more considerate, and to ignore any kind of issue. Ehlert exercises introversion. The young pilot who has aged years at the forest camp has to experience many human shortcomings during the everyday life of the camp. Much meanness manifests itself here, right up to the basest behaviour. There are thefts and cabals, and there is informing. The Russian camp command sells some of the provisions, clothes and shoes to the civilian population, which is suffering almost as much as the German prisoners during this winter. After half a year only 110 out of 500 prisoners are fit for work due to malnutrition.

Ehlert senses a new attitude to the Germans in the Russians: the prisoners are to rebuild what they destroyed in the Soviet Union. And he is able to observe that the former members of the National Committee, which was dissolved in autumn 1945, try once again to trim their sails to the wind. Many of those who for months received perks because of their alleged political reformation do not want to hear of this now.

'It was not that good, either, I was taken for a ride, in fact it was utter nonsense, I can hardly believe that I took part in this.' Such sentences can be heard everywhere in the camp. Those who remained steadfast and did not sell their souls listen to this whitewashing with smirks.

It might be the end of April or the beginning of May 1947 when Ehlert and a large part of the forest camp at Bolshoy Bor are transferred to a principal camp at Seloni-Dolsk near Kazan. Like most of his comrades, he is too weak to continue the hard labour in the forest.

During the first days the men have to listen to speeches each morning during roll call, according to which the Soviet Union is making headway again, Hitler's Germany is lying broken until doomsday and the German prisoners of war have to perform reconstruction work. They all will go home soon, if they just work diligently enough.

The anniversary of the German surrender, 8 May, is celebrated for two days. During clothes muster a few days later the Russians notice Ehlert's shoddy footwear. The old Russian felt boots are reduced to mere tatters. His toes, around which he has wrapped just a few rags, show painful burst blisters. He receives peculiar canvas shoes: an oval board onto which canvas cloth is nailed all around. Every day he now trudges to work in these and wherever else he has to go. He takes off this footwear only for sleeping. It is well that it is not far to the quarry where he has to work now. With time he gets used to the shoes. He takes comfort in the fact that others are stuck with such shoes, too.

The worst happens on the second day though. The men have to march through town to the communal baths. It takes them one and a half hours. Along the way the boards of Ehlert's shoes torture him so much that he believes he would be better off walking barefoot. He has a sore spot on his foot when they finally reach town. Inside the bath they meet numerous German captives from other camps. All their body hair is removed before entering the showers. The razor used is fortunately not as blunt as the first times. Yet again they are standing in front of uniformed Russian women. The first brushes a little water on their chests. Next to her are four women with razors pulling out and shaving off the prisoners' hair. Only their beards are left alone. It is pure torture. As usual, the men then are pinched on the bottom by a female doctor – the customary method to determine who still has some meat on their ribs.

Of course, all of them are declared fit for work. The provisions here are slightly better than at the forest camp. Two German chefs are on duty and they try their best each day with 600g bread and half a litre of soup three time a day. Now, even at lunchtime, Ehlert and his comrades get soup in the camp, on two occasions even additional gruel. And at some point a veritable feast for the prisoners occurs: one Friday each receives a few chunks of American tinned meat. The basics for the food in Seloni-Dolsk remain the same as at the forest camp, however: cabbage, potatoes, flour, millet, gruel, oats or buckwheat, and additionally some fat or oil. Since the soup only contains a few drops of grease at best, the Russians give the order to distribute the fat or oil for each portion separately. Every prisoner now receives his measure of fat in his soup with a thimble on a stick.

As can be felt by the provision of the food, the situation for the German prisoners relaxes a little. Mortality drops in those days, and Ehlert even gains a little weight. At the beginning they receive their entire bread ration in the evening, but some of the smokers exchange half their ration with a non-smoker for the latter's tobacco allowance, which belongs to the rations here. This is soon noticed by the Russian camp command. As a result, one weak man is ordered to cut the bread. He has to hand out exactly 200g bread per meal to each prisoner, and it has to be eaten together with the soup. As long as this is monitored, all is well, but when the supervision ceases, the bread and tobacco trade resumes immediately.

In this way Ehlert often has an additional 200g of bread and that starts to show. Ehlert reflects that if this was a regular occurrence, then it would be bearable, although he still feels hungry after each meal. He actually cannot explain to himself why he still feels hungry after each meal, but it is a fact. The food is simply not filling enough. And this does not remain regular. Often there is nothing but tea *or* bread *or* soup for one or two days, depending on what arrives at the camp. Such is the case with Christmas 1947. The weather is very cold, there is no bread and only very thin soup. During evening roll call the Russian camp commander says: '*Saftra budit cleb*' (tomorrow there will be bread). Yet no bread arrives for five days. On the second day the German camp commander says: 'Today is Christmas Eve, and we will all go to the mess hall.' There, roughly 200 men have space to stand, while the others stand in the corridor of the large barracks. The camp commander gives a short speech, and it is completely quiet and solemn in the room. Then 'Silent night' is intoned. All immediately join in, but during the phrase 'all asleep, lonely wakes' many of the men's voices falter, and tears flow. For many these are the first tears during their captivity. The song is finished with slightly stifled voices. This is one of the Christmas celebrations Ehlert will always remember. Not a single Russian is to be seen though. This evening, there is only tea, the same on Christmas morning, again just tea without bread. After that they go to the quarry.

One day here is like another. When they set off from the camp, the chefs ask the men to gather wood waste. They do not have wood left for their fires. However, the prisoners have already collected everything loose during the previous days, and that day there is hardly anything left. The Russians know this, but do not do anything about it. They understand that the prisoners celebrate Christmas on these days, but they do not make life easier because of it. On Boxing Day, which passes by almost unnoticed, one of the men mentions that food has arrived once more, but the chefs have no wood left for cooking. The forest is only a kilometre away, but the Russians insist that they have no permission to fetch wood out there. It is allegedly a capital offence to cut wood. When it gets dark, however, two Russian guard posts enter the barracks and look for the German camp senior. He is to assign thirty men to fetch wood after all. After an hour the men return to the camp, each laden with a beam. Sometimes two men carry an especially heavy piece. The wood has to be cut and chopped immediately. Since the kitchen is only equipped with one saw and one axe, it takes until morning until the wood is ready.

The guards and the thirty men carried away an entire line-keeper's lodge from the rail tracks far away and then brought it to the camp in its components. The chefs heap praise on the dry timber, as it burns like tinder. Early in the morning they already have soup and gruel. In contrast, the bread from the factory only arrives on the fifth day. Then each prisoner promptly receives a whole tin loaf, and some of the men devour it in one go until their bellies ache.

After a few months Ehlert is transferred from Seloni-Dolsk near Kazan to Zaporozhye. This will turn out to be a lucky break. After Yelabuga, Zaporozhye is the best camp of his time in captivity. This is due to the humanity of the Russian camp command. Politics hardly play a role. The last year, 1949, is quite bearable for the prisoners. Many have regained their normal weight, are allowed to receive mail, to write as much as they want and to have packages sent to them.

Only Gerhard Ehlert remains in silence. He has not heard anything from home, from Riele, for a long time. He distracts himself with cultural events. The men have a winner in their Russian cultural officer and every Sunday he demands a cultural performance of the drama group, the choir and the orchestra. 'But only if there is no work.'

And so the prisoners discuss what to do for the next half a year. Ehlert plays in the orchestra – the only third violin, as there are no violas. There are a few professional musicians in the party, which totals fifteen members. Among the fellow players is Heinz Zander, who was born in 1925 and is an exceptionally gifted music student from Cologne. He plays cello and piano, and every now and again accordion, too. The conductor of the small orchestra is Walter Heier from Leipzig. He is thirty-five years old and a music master, the best of his year, who was fortunate enough to have studied at the renowned Berlin Academy of Music. He has excellent hearing and can notate musical pieces from memory. This is important, since there are no scores. Heier writes at a table without the aid of a piano. He provides a wide range of hit songs, from popular music to Beethoven's *7th Symphony*. Among the musicians is a solo pianist from Leipzig Radio who still knows Beethoven's *1st Piano Concerto* by heart. Heier notates the orchestral parts for it and it is actually performed.

The majority of the officers belonging to the cultural squad are kept in one dorm, the 'culture dorm' and they stay together until the dissolution of the camp in 1949. All other dorms are mixed up about four times a year in order to prevent conspirational cabals. Also in the culture dorm is Wolfgang Buddenberg, aged thirty-six, who is a circuit judge from Westphalia; a short, slender man with a great sense of humour. He will later become a federal judge. He contributes much to the entertainment with sketches. His great success is the libretto for an operetta, *Cleopatra's Pearls*. Heinz Zander composes the music. Ehlert often watches him at his work and he writes at a crazy pace. The other musicians copy their parts from his score: everything fits. For paper they use the two inner layers of the four-layer cement bags – the outer layers are too dirty. The men have to draw staves and treble clefs constantly.

Cleopatra's Pearls becomes a great success and is performed several times at the culture club. In addition the orchestra plays the operetta *Blue Mask* (Maske in Blau). Ehlert establishes a string quartet with three other musicians. They practise for a year and then perform a quartet evening called 'Eine kleine Nachtmusik' (A little night music, the name of Mozart's *Serenade No. 13*). It is announced by a huge poster and the club is, of course, jam-packed for the performance. The string quartet plays eight short pieces, among them a composition by Ehlert that he jotted down during Advent 1944. Between the musical pieces Hans Korte, a merchant from Hamburg, recites matching poems.

As well as shorter labour deployments, Ehlert is employed at three work stations during these weeks: at a brickworks, an oil mill, and the construction site of a theatre. At the latter he suffers an accident in September 1949 during the casting of a concrete ceiling. While pushing a wheelbarrow full of concrete, the wheelbarrow overturns and hits his body. He plunges from up high and hits the ground on his back. His friend Wigand Wüster shouts for help. A horse-drawn cart drives Ehlert back to the camp, where he has to be supported by two medics. Without them he immediately slumps to the ground. The Russian female doctor feels his spinal column and says she cannot find an injury. However, an X-ray three years later will discover that one of the lumbar vertebrae had been broken, but has fully healed in the meantime. As a result, Ehlert is officially assessed as war affected by 30 per cent. In fact, he narrowly avoided paraplegia.

Ehlert came to Zaporozhye with 500 other officers – to a camp previously occupied by the German lower ranks. However, the Russians soon realise that they have to treat the officers differently. First the new 'guests' complain that glass is missing from the windows of several dorms. Then they demand to carry out the first month of labour without normal requirements because they are not used to it. This insubordination displeases the Russian camp command so much that they have the Germans' spokesman, a cavalry captain called Eichhorn of the 24th Tank Division, transferred to another camp. The prisoners immediately commence a strike that lasts until he is returned. This attitude delights the lower ranks, too. It catches on so much that the Russians do not dare to enter some dorms.

During these days the camp holds 1,500 men, including the officers. The German camp commander, who as a Communist has even been in a concentration camp, is the only diehard socialist. Around another 100 travel in his political wake. They become typists, work in the kitchen or in the bakery. The rest openly face up to the socialist regime. Time and again men are put into punishment details. This means working every Sunday, too.

Nevertheless, Ehlert perceives his time at Zaporozhye as not too bad. One of his duties is to supply the loam for the brickworks. Five men are allocated to one dram, which has to be shovelled full and then driven to the pits slightly downhill. If the production at the brickworks comes to a standstill, the men have a break. The work can be easily done by four men so that one of them can always have a break. After three months Ehlert is at peace. Politics only plays a minor role now. What is more, no further attempts at re-education are made. His political file has grown thicker though. The punishment for that is still to follow.

8

One of the Last

In Zaporozhye, 1949 is the year of the discharges. The first transports to Germany are arranged at some point – mostly the seriously ill who almost all have to be carted off on stretchers and be loaded onto the train carriages. Of these, only a few will arrive home alive. Inside the camp a market for German places of domicile is evolving at that time, a kind of home exchange: everybody who wants to be discharged has to name a home address. There are three groups without addresses. The largest are prisoners who had their home in the newly founded German Democratic Republic, but due to their experiences in the Soviet Union want to go west, i.e. to the Federal Republic. The second group comprises the East Prussians, whose homeland no longer belongs to Germany. The smallest group are the West Germans who were too deeply involved in the National Committee during their captivity. These men do not want or do not dare to return to their West German home. All have one thing in common: they urgently need a home address. 'Don't you have an aunt or anybody else to whom I can travel?' is a frequently posed question. And many a prisoner thus acquires a whole new family at this exchange.

Ehlert becomes more and more nervous during these days in November 1949. By this time he is among the last hundred of the formerly 1,500 men in the Zaporozhye camp. Every day a small Russian steps out of the barracks with a slip of paper and reads out a few names – men who have the luck to be allowed to pack their belongings. They are driven to the station on a truck. Or he reads the names of the prisoners who have been sentenced to twenty-five years of forced labour and from now on are no longer classified as prisoners of war, but as war criminals. Two men from Ehlert's dorm bring the condemned their daily food rations and describe the mood among those men, which ranges from depression, total indifference, apathy to gallows humour.

Every day a round dozen of names are read out, sometimes even more. Ehlert's name is never among them. He does not understand why he is not allowed to return home. His aviator colleagues have long since been called out. Bomber pilots who wreaked far more havoc on enemy territory than he did with camera and a flashlight made their return journey long ago. Every day the number of prisoners is dwindling, and Ehlert takes fright. His only comfort is that his best friend – actually his only friend – is still in the camp, too. Wigand Wüster's name has not been on any list so far, either. They are thus still together.

It continues in this vein for six weeks; six bloody long, nerve-wrecking weeks. They cause him the greatest emotional stress of his entire captivity. Will he remain in Russia forever? Will he never see his home again? How often has he posed these questions to himself. Yet never have they tortured him so much as now. And then, two days before Christmas, Wigand Wüster's name is on the list, too, together with his own. They are on the lucky list. For the first time in his life, Leutnant Gerhard Ehlert has tears in his eyes.

For his trip home he receives a new wardrobe. He gets a brand new Wehrmacht jacket – of course without rank insignia. From where did the Russians get these, four years after the war? No matter! He is on his way home. Yet beforehand come the usual examinations. Once again he and the other dozen men have to present themselves naked in front of the Russian doctors. They are certainly not pleasing sights with their emaciated bodies, Ehlert thinks, and hopes at the same moment that nobody has heard his thoughts. He does not want any last-minute trouble.

Then they are shepherded to the point where the transport is assembled. Both of them walk with the other returnees to the station. The livestock wagons have been cleaned and fitted with benches – and for the first time they remain unlocked. Since it is cold, each wagon has a potbelly stove. This is fed with 2m-long logs. As the wood is moist, it takes a long time until they catch fire.

The returnees are only allowed one tin spoon. Knives and forks are prohibited as they can be used as weapons. Since most of them smoke, they were at least able to pack matches. It takes a lot of cutting and splicing to finally get a fire started. Before their departure the Russian camp commander goes from wagon to wagon to ask after the men's state. For every wagon a senior is appointed immediately after loading. This person has to report to the camp commander, a Russian colonel, whether or not everything is in order. The commander goes from wagon to wagon and indeed receives reports in each.

Then the wagons start to roll and this time in the right direction: west. They depart at dawn. The men are permitted to alight when the train halts.

They are even allowed to leave the train at train stations. Some captives who are still light on their feet visit the bazaar in one town to barter pieces of clothing against food. One man exchanges a woollen blanket he received in place of a coat against groceries. As a result he catches pneumonia, because it is too cold without his blanket. On the whole the men are sufficiently clothed for the return journey. There is also good and ample food during the transport so that it is more bearable than any of the camps.

Brest-Litovsk is the border station between Russia and Poland. A thorough search is carried out one last time. Photos are taken away from the men, but they receive packages of tea and tobacco in return. Everyone grabs what he can. And then there is a final check: arms up! Once again the Russians hunt for SS members. This sends a jolt of fear through Wigand Wüster, who has had a skin discolouration since early childhood. White patches manifest all over his body. During the check he is flagged, as the guards suspect that he has cut out his SS tattoo. Yet then a doctor is consulted and he frees Wüster from suspicion. The latter's shock is so deep that he is hardly responsive during the following days.

Finally the train rolls slowly through Poland, stopping here and there. Poles approach the Germans again and again, and their hatred for the Russians is obvious. The latter have taken much of their territory and driven 1½ million people from their homelands. At night the Poles blow up train tracks.

Ehlert is reminded of the partisan war against the German Wehrmacht. He once witnessed how at an airfield in Poland, an entire crew boarding a plane was shot by Polish snipers without the airfield security being able to interfere. From then on there had been a fear of snipers. And now the Russians do not dare to enter the forests at night. The victors do not trust the victors.

On they travel until they finally reach German territory. The train drives slowly, so slowly that men can run alongside and beg. They ask for cigarettes and food. Yet the returnees have only very little themselves. And then they hear voices that touch them to the core. For the first time in years they hear the voices of German children. How foreign they sound, Ehlert thinks.

In Frankfurt on the Oder speeches are addressed to the returnees. All have to sign a resolution: 'Never again war against the Soviet Union!' Of course, all are in agreement. Ehlert hastily sends a telegram home that he is on his way and the approximate time he will arrive at the reception camp in Friedland. From Frankfurt onwards they only travel at night. In Heiligenstadt they rest under the roof of a school. Again they need to wait for nightfall. Then they travel by train to Arenshausen and from there 3km on foot to the inner German border, where Ehlert arrives late in the evening.

It is New Year's Eve 1949. The inner German border runs along the entrance to the Besenhausen estate. Five Soviet officers are standing on the road there, and 10m farther along are five British officers. Only when they reach the British officers are they convinced that their captivity has come to an end. A few metres along a tall nun is standing in the middle of the road. She tries to shake each prisoner's hand. It is like a warm salute from heaven, Ehlert muses. And their luck does not end there. Fifty metres farther down the road is the Salvation Army. The men receive a mug of heavenly hot chocolate and a sandwich. For the returnees from Russia, these are two wholly unfamiliar items of food. So this is the West, Ehlert thinks to himself.

9

Stranger at Home

From Busse the journey continues to the reception camp at Friedland, and there the young soldier returning home after five years of captivity experiences his first disappointment: nobody has come to welcome him. Not his parents nor Riele, from whom he has not heard anything in a long time. Nobody has come, although his home town, Göttingen, is virtually around the corner. Three men are from Göttingen: Wigand Wüster, Gerhard Ehlert and a non-commissioned officer. The latter's wife has come with a three-wheel car to fetch her husband. Incredible scenes of reunion take place, which make Ehlert sad.

After a short introduction, during which they get to know each other a little and draw confidence, the non-commissioned officer offers Ehlert a ride home. Ehlert climbs onto the open truck of the three-wheeler and Wüster travels in another vehicle. The former alights in the village of Geismar, where Ehlert's parents have been living after they left the barracks. He wants to go the last metres on foot. On his way he encounters a few drunks, as it is New Year's Eve.

Yet Ehlert has no stomach at all for celebration right now. All his thoughts are focussed on the freedom for which he had to wait so long. Finally he can go where he wants without guards. He thinks mournfully of those who had to remain behind. How could he be merry at this thought. So he observes the revellers with some astonishment. Then he enters a strange house in which he is supposed to live from now on. Finally free!

His captivity has come to an end. And yet Ehlert is beset by a kind of melancholy at that moment. Never again will he have the opportunity to look into the deepest degradation of the human soul. Never again will he get to know such a range of people from all walks of life, who reveal their admirable or despicable character as soon as the naked beast emerges from under the thin layer of civilisation. Ehlert has got to know great people and unprincipled bastards, and he had to realise that most men are cowards when tested to their core.

Never again will he have the opportunity to meet people who due to their position within the camp ruthlessly converted so much food for their own use that they could barter with it, while others starved. When the mass of the prisoners was all skin and bones, this group often showed a little belly so that they were called 'piggies'. Many would have lived their lives unblemished during normal times, Ehlert knows in this moment shortly before freedom. In the exceptional situation of captivity they were too weak to do so. This applied to all types of professions, also those to which moral fortitude is usually ascribed. Judges, priests and doctors became traitors and thieves. Humans are humans, Ehlert thinks. You have to be prepared for or anticipate anything. Yet there were also shining counter-examples, demonstrations of courage and truthfulness, of magnanimity, of selfless altruism that he will remember with gratitude. For example, those Red Army soldiers who played music with him at the command post, who fed Burr and him and treated them both like friends. 'Just help yourself and eat – I know you are hungry', the Siberian said to him. Friends in war. But after all, the Russian stole the German pilot's boots. Enemies in war.

And Ehlert has to think of the head of a guard detail who consistently made life easier for the prisoners. As soon as one of his superiors showed up in the wider vicinity of the Germans, the Russian guard raged and ranted – winking knowingly at them during his display. As soon as Comrade Political Officer had vanished, he grinned at the prisoners and told them to resume work – but at a leisurely pace. Sometimes he even added the only German word they taught him: '*Pause* [breaktime]!'

Ehlert has to think of a poor Russian girl too, that naive chit who fell in love with one of the young prisoners during an external camp detachment. But no external detachment lasts forever. No prisoner remains where he is deployed forever. The girl stood in front of the gate to the camp for days. At some point she asked for her German, whereupon she was arrested on the spot and led away. Which camp has she vanished into, probably forever?

Then he experiences the most terrible hour of his freedom, which even eclipses the worst hours in captivity. There is no embrace for the returnee, no warm welcome. He does not even hear the phrase: 'How are you?' For the first time it would have had meaning in the young man's life. A chilly atmosphere prevails. The beloved son no longer exists for those who stayed home.

A stranger has come through the door. During the following days Ehlert will not receive a single card, letter or flower bouquet as a welcome from anybody. Only one aunt writes a few lines: 'It is wonderful that you have your soldier back.' She writes this to his parents, not to him. Riele has grown apart from him, too. It will take months for Ehlert, the former night-time reconnaissance pilot of the Luftwaffe, Stalin's prisoner, to find his way back to his family. To Riele. Months full of agony as a stranger at home.

Epilogue

He looks elegant, fine-limbed and well-dressed. When I stand for the first time before the short, delicate man, I know very well that I only have a single chance. One false sentence, one stupid question and my introduction will have been ruined forever and he will shut himself off from me. This is what I have almost always found with many former Second World War soldiers whom I have interviewed in recent years: they want to open themselves up, but their story is so important to them that they want to be taken seriously as well. They have great suspicion of those who were not there, who have no idea what it feels like to have sacrificed one's youth for a senseless, evil idea. They are suspicious of those who have their knowledge of that time from history books and have never looked death in the eyes during war themselves. Of those who in their opinion do not know how it is to have been seduced by the dark power of a hitherto unknown quality and have suffered for it.

And Gerhard Ehlert is their prime example. The 92-year-old speaks a polished German, is highly alert and is able to explain technical correlations in every detail at any time – and that in well-worded sentences. The Wehrmacht officer is still in him, that is evident from his gestures, his posture, his succinct language. He is still living in his parental home without dependence on outside assistance. He looks at me and my journalist's untrained physique with disparaging glances and during my first visit presses a sheet of paper into my hand on which are printed ten exercises that I should perform. 'I do this daily, And you ought to do this training too, otherwise you will walk with a stick in a few years,' the old gentleman says with a smile, but in the firm tone of a well-meant order given to a fifty-year-old.

For days we sit together in his house, which is just a few kilometres from the Baltic Sea bay, and do not notice the time of the day when it slowly grows darker outside. We forget to switch on the light. Ehlert recounts his story without pause. In between he fetches one or other memento from another room, shows photographs or stands at the window. We have only met each other a few weeks ago and yet have become familiar quite quickly, although Ehlert would never allow even a modicum of intimacy. He is too genteel, has never learned to be on first-name terms and does not wish to learn this now. It would not suit him, either.

A colleague from the Rosenheimer publishing company to whom Ehlert's story was proposed, but who at that time had to work on another biography, entrusted him to me, this elderly slim gentleman from Western Pomerania who had a very special task during the Second World War: to count tanks, artillery, trucks, soldiers and trains from the air during night.

Infantrymen, tank soldiers, pioneers, mountain troopers, men in the Africa Korps, artillery soldiers, communication officers and drivers – their fates exist in the millions, and although no less interesting they have already been documented on an epic scale. The story of a night-time reconnaissance pilot, who in autumn 1944 flies with his twin-engine aircraft through the dark and without on-board radar into the heart of the downfall of Army Group Centre and is shot down behind enemy lines, fascinates me right from the start – just as does the man himself and his colourful family history. His was a typical German fate by the way, which shows how people from all walks of life let themselves be ensnared by the Third Reich. I have incorporated the detailed historical passages concerning the Ehlert family not without reason. They mark out their ensnarement into the web of the Nazi empire.

Ehlert's nadir in his history as a soldier in the Second World War was not the crash of his aircraft, which he was extremely lucky to survive, not the deaths of his comrades, not his captivity, which pushed the young pilot to his limits at times. No, it was his return home as a stranger. After years of war and captivity, to be treated like a stranger by his loved ones – that was his personal low-water mark. Yet even this Gerhard Ehlert has mastered, survived like the crash of his plane over Russia. He remained persistent, studied and established his own company as a construction engineer. With great success. And he fought his way back to his personal happiness, too. Gabriele 'Riele' Müller, who had grown apart from him during the years of his captivity, was won back by him. She became his wife, and the two of them lived happily together until her death a few years ago. Ehlert is a father and grandfather, and his grandchildren listen to him when he tells his story 'from heaven to hell'.

Wasserburg on the Inn, autumn 2014
Christian Huber

About the Author

Christian Huber, born in 1964 in Wasserburg on the Inn, has been working as a journalist and writer for twenty years. His specialised subject is contemporary history. After studying at Munich University, he published numerous series and reports on the Second World War as editor of the *Oberbayerisches Volksblatt* newspaper, where he worked for fifteen years. The former fixed-term professional soldier and retired captain completed his military training, among other places, at the officer candidate school of the Luftwaffe in Fürstenfeldbruck.

Huber is currently living and working as an independent journalist and author in Wasserburg.